# Who and Where is God ?

## The search that has led Humanity to violence

## Dr. Ursula M. Anderson

RESOURCE *Publications* • Eugene, Oregon

Resource Publications
A division of Wipf and Stock Publishers
199 W 8th Ave, Suite 3
Eugene, OR 97401

Who and Where Is God?
The Search That Has Led Humanity to Violence
By Anderson, Ursula M., MD
Copyright©2007 by Anderson, Ursula M., MD
ISBN 13: 978-1-61097-080-8
Publication date 10/27/2010
Previously published by Infinity Publishing, 2007

# *Table of Contents*

# *Acknowledgments*

Each of my recent books which with this one now number four, emerged from the same lineage of concern for the escalation of violence throughout the world, and in particular among the young. Each in its own way describes the pivotal role that *memory*, both personal and trans-generational has played in the evolution of human *consciousness*, and how both play out in human feelings and behavior. Overall, they issue an invitation to re-think whom we are and how we came to be whom we are. *Who and Where is God?* goes further by exposing the beliefs and attitudes that have blighted the divine within our human nature. In so doing, it gives promise to what we may become if we put our hands to the plough of tending the soil of the communal human soul. Such knowledge comes from the interplay of many energies; intuition, observation, people, places, books, art, music, customs, to mention but a few. Throughout my journey, they have been my constant companions and all, in one way or another, have been my teachers. So, I acknowledge and give thanks for their tutelage of the ways of light and dark. They were, in fact, gifts of the One, Eternal, and Holy Spirit who travels with us all and who is therefore, the source of my knowledge and the recipient of my gratitude.

And to the countless children and their families world wide, whose love and struggles became a part of my knowing and gave me the inspiration for this and several of my other books, I give my loving gratitude.

Finally to Daniel Horner, who transcribed my hand written text into a readable and computer friendly manuscript, and to Heather Oberg, who greatly assisted in producing the cover, I give my sincere gratitude and I wish them many blessings along the paths of their lives.

# Prologue

It was a dull and rainy day in Godsall, a dear little seaside town on the south coast of England. Needing to purchase a few morsels I had traveled there by bus to escape the Saturday crowds in the bustling city of Brighton where I was staying, which make of the simplest task of shopping there an exercise in survival. Walking through the pedestrianized shopping center in Godsall, I noticed an inviting little café, so, feeling the need to rest a while, I walked in to get a spot of that wonderful beverage that puts starch into even the most jaded of human beings. It was tea-time so many other people had the same idea as myself. Looking around I saw that the only seat available was one half of a lovely old wooden bench, the other half being occupied by a man who was smoking a cigarette and drinking a latte cappuccino, the latter surely being a transgression on the sacredness of English tea-time.

"May I sit down," I asked. "Of course, if you don't mind my smoking." Well, gasping for a cup of tea and with nowhere else to park myself, I had no choice, so down I sat. As the tea percolated its task of perking me up and the coffee latte doing the same for him, our conversation began to bubble.

At one point, and I suppose, when he felt safe with this stranger at his side, he asked, "Have you ever wondered WHY in all religions men control the issues and make the laws while women, who really keep these religions going, are never consulted but are expected to obey the rules when as is so often the case, they rule against them?" Hardly believing what I heard I replied; "It is truly amazing that you should ask me such a question, because I have not only thought about it a lot but I am currently writing a book about it and related issues.

Would you like to hear a little of what I have to say?"

"I'd love to."

*Well, nut-shelling a vast topic, the creative soul of WOMAN, which is her true identity, was stolen by ideas and belief systems codified in religious scriptures written by men which have become intertwined with cultural beliefs and practices. This intertwining led to the development of hierarchies and practices that elevated the male to positions of superiority and power and assigned women and their children to roles of inferiority and subservience.*

*These beliefs and practices have throughout the past three millennia and maybe longer, become deeply entrenched in the collective memory and consciousness of people and their cultures all over the world. Like all victims who have had their unique and sacred identities trampled and stolen, women to survive, played the roles thrust upon them by their victimizers and the male hegemony that stole their identity and freedom from them.*

Ruminating on what I had said for several moments, he said, "You know, what you say makes a lot of sense and what you said about 'belief systems' is so right; they really rule us and if that promotes love and tolerance that is good, but if not, it creates divisions. Like for example myself, I vote Labour and I can be in a group of people feeling fine and enjoying what each one has to say – until – I discover that one of them votes Conservative! Immediately, I can feel my whole attitude changing almost to the point of perceiving that person as an enemy. Then when I realize what has happened I say to myself; "For God's sake why can't I, and everyone else for that matter, see others as human beings traveling similar journeys and set aside the differences of beliefs that divide us;" sentiments to which I said a loud "AMEN." Returning to the question he initially posed I added to what I had already said that history tells us that Religion and Culture were not always structured the way they are today. Research has shown that prior to the scriptures that gave precedence to the male, it appears that humanity centered around WOMAN as Birther, Nurturer, and Crone, and I touch on this history in this and other books I have authored.

I bless that man whose name I don't know but who through the questions he posed, provided me with a heartfelt and simple introduction to the subject this book attempts to address:

Who and Where is God?

The answer to which must surely provide insight into why we humans are the way we are.

And just for the record, I have always believed in angels and that sometimes they fold their wings and appear in human form. Some as I found out, even smoke cigarettes and drink coffee at English tea-time.

Oh my. SUCH HERETICAL BRAVADO

But Oh, WHAT A GIFT.

# I

# The Sacred Webs of Memory and Consciousness

Spring comes late to Western New York where I live, but each year the grackles and robins, along with the doves and barn swallows arrive back from their winter abodes. Their arrival in mid-to-late March is always a heart-warming event, heralding as it does the arrival of spring. Some take up residence under the eaves of the roof, others nest on top of the pillars as they jut out from underneath the porches they support, and others choose the barn as well as other places including the old milk shed and well house. From dawn to dusk these creatures are madly busy either repairing the vacated nests of their ancestors, some of which may have been their own birthing places and nurseries, or, as the severity of our winters often make necessary, building new ones. Then they all get down to the business of mating and raising their fledglings. Some of these families offer me an opportunity to participate in their rituals for it is not uncommon for the greedy young ones to fall out of their nest when they have overreached in order to retrieve food from the beaks of their parents. These little fallen ones either get returned to the nest or, if the parents have flown away, I nurture them until they can fly away on their own life's journey, but with the memories of their beginnings safely tucked away under their wings to be replicated next year and the next and the next.

Just like the swallows, who every year at dawn on March 19th, St. Joseph's day, begin to arrive at the centuries old mission of San Juan Capistrano in Southern California, to build their nests or repair those of yesteryear. Through the sunny summer days they mate, raise their young and then unfailingly on October 23rd, the feast of St. Juan Capistrano, the swallows, parents and children alike, take flight to their winter habitats in the southern hemisphere.

The sagas of nature's rituals are endless. The salmon in our streams - yes, we have them in Western New York - often make heroic journeys back to the place where they were spawned and where they, like their ancestors, will spend themselves spawning new life that will ensure the continuance of their kind into endless future generations. These and other wondrous happenings throughout and within creation have always intrigued and challenged humanity. Their precision and repetition, their inherent beauty and thrust to survival and reproduction, jostle with questions that beg knowledge of how it is all accomplished.

Obviously, *memory*, in particular some trans-generational aspects of it and other yet unnamed factors, drive these phenomena. But, then, one has to ask what is it that drives and directs memory with such power and elegance. Our lives and customs are engulfed by memory. The rituals and liturgies of religion and the rites of human passage are chosen for their significance in the lives of past generations, vehicles within which we feel, know, and even touch our connectedness as a continuum with all existence. As an entity, *memory* has been the subject of much discourse throughout recorded history, discourse which has reached a crescendo of speculation and definition over the past quarter century; but, its precise nature continues to elude us. To enumerate the functions of *memory* is to state the obvious. It overlaps with our perceptions and often directs, in a sense, our ability to learn. It flows into and interacts with our consciousness at all of its levels, thus providing the stage, if not also the choreography, for the unfolding drama of our lives. The ancient Greeks knew this. They regarded their goddess Mnemosyne as the fount of *memory* and the mother of the muses. They believed that poetry, song, and drama, indeed, every creative art form, sprang from memory and would forever be rooted in it. Moreover, they believed that *memory* was the "all" of life and that, therefore, all creation was her offspring; but from where, beyond Mnemosyne, did memory arise?

Aeschylus, the great Greek philosopher, asserted that *memory* was the mother of all wisdom. However, in the Judaic scriptures of his time, wisdom is referred to as "she" who was before all creation. If so, then who and what is *memory* if she is the mother of wisdom and progenitor and transmitter of life? Pursuing her identity was for millennia the purview of philosophers and poets, a pursuit she artfully eluded with only the barest of holes in her veils. During the latter half of the 20th century scientists joined the pursuit, but put an emphasis on finding a precise location wherein she dwells. One has to wonder at the logic behind this, not only because *memory* is so pervasive in our lives but, because findings from sociological research makes it clear that describing location defines the inhabitants thereof in only the most general of terms. This approach, however, is in tune with the thrust of most Western science which tends to describe phenomena by the variables associated with them, as well as in terms of their secondary characteristics of form and function rather than of their essence. Scientific sleuthing after *memory* has proceeded along two pathways and their attendant parameters. On the one hand, neurobiologists who assume that *memory* is solely a function of the brain have tried to establish its hardware by tracking the nerve cells and their neurons involved to some degree with one or another of its numerous functions. On the other hand, psychologists have been probing the software of *memory* by attempting to describe its many facets and functions. One of their most important conclusions was arrived at by studying patients with varying degrees and modes of loss of memory, collectively referred to as amnesia. From this, they concluded that there is no single entity that can be called *memory*. How correct they are can be confirmed by a few moments reflection on whom we are and how we came to be. For example, in all species when an egg is fertilized, and providing it escapes threats to its development, it will eventually be born as a replica of its parent(s). At the time of fertilization, there is no brain and, therefore, no road map of nerve cells and neurons to enable its inherent *memory* of who it is, to proceed through the growth and development that culminates in it replicating its progenitors. In fact, so certain are we that this elusive entity, called *memory*, will reproduce its own kind, we rarely give it a thought in the begetting of our own children. Likewise, when mice and other mammalians are bred in research laboratories, it never occurs to us that a mouse might produce an elephant or that an elephant and other species in the wild would reproduce anything other than their own kind. Surely then, it is obvious that *memory* by any other name is not only within and at the very heart and center of creation, but goes before it in all of its manifestations.

*Memory is primal to our existence.*

Furthermore, recent advances in neurophysiology have delineated some of the orderly electrochemical and energy bases of how we function. That these are transmitted trans-generationally confirms what perennial wisdom has always known; all life and its sustaining functions are encoded in *memory* and, therefore, *memory* is everywhere within the body and soul, not just in one place. We come into life because of *memory* and its legions of specificities for each and every trait of whom we are and may become, contained within the energies of our genes and other energy systems that accompany them. A half century ago Albert Einstein told us that ultimate reality lay within fields of energy and not within matter, regardless how small its particles. Thus, while we still conceive of genes as particulate matter which, indeed they are, we know the driving force behind their activities must be energy. We know, too, that all functions of our mind, body, and soul are affected through fields of electrochemical magnetic energy which, in fact, form the bases for many medical diagnostic tests. But, since all life is encoded in *memory*, then *memory* is also energy. We also know that energy fields are acutely sensitive to all that disturbs or threatens their particular functional frequencies and wave patterns and when this happens, it changes the nature of their activities to the point of their dysfunction.[1]

*Memory* operates within our beings in a manner akin to how the physical immune system functions. The cells of the immune system, the substances they produce, and their receptors throughout the body are thinking entities whose function is to defend against all that is non-self through a system of locks and keys that for the most part operates with exquisite precision and protectiveness. Sadly, there are times when the immune system dysfunctions. In some cases, it overreacts to external stimuli, e.g., in allergies and autoimmune diseases, and in others, it fails to react or it under-reacts. In all cases, the

[1] Ursula M. Anderson, *The Sacredness of Memory: Immunology and the Soul.* ANIMA (Buffalo Diocesan Liturgical Commission: Buffalo, NY), (XV11, No. 2, 1993): 1314 (11-19 -The full article may be obtained by contacting She-Bear Publications, P. O. Box 503, Ellicottville, NY 14731).

*memory* sequences of how to protect the body temple have been injured, and the precise sensitivity of that energy damaged to where it no longer can function as it was intended. The confusion and anger at this betrayal of self and self-identity is manifested by disease, dysfunction, and disorder.

Wondrous as all of this is, how did it get started? Eschewing for a moment the mythology that surrounds Judeo-Christian biblical accounts of Creation, scientists tell us that at the beginning there was a horrendous collision of forces in the universe that liberated atoms of carbon, hydrogen, nitrogen, and oxygen, a happening that is now referred to as the "Big Bang." Over time, these elements engaged each other in the primal dance of creation. From their various unions emerged several variations of the arrangements they made for coexistence, no doubt in each instance getting it right after much trial and error. The molecules so formed continued to dance in ever-escalating complexity to form the building blocks that over millennia became the infrastructure and basis of plant life and uni-cellular organisms - all eventually evolving into the human form.

At every step of the way, constant adjustments had to be made not only to permit the wondrous diversity and healthy unfolding of species-specific life, but also to allow for responses to the environments within which they were made in order to permit continuance of life itself. It is a dialogue that continues to this day, but within which environment is presently taking on the more talkative and dominant role, which is not always beneficial. The greed for money and the lust for consumerism that it generates have led to the mindless rape and destruction of land and forests and the pollution of air and water all of which challenge the memories of healthy function and could compromise the gifts of creation that sustain life. Pitting this negative trend against the majesty of creation that has brought us to where we are, one prays and works for it to be halted and stopped in its tracks. Glimmers of the march that is the unfolding of creation are evident throughout recorded history and in the 20th century described in compelling and deeply spiritual terms by the great paleontologist and priest Pierre Teilhard de Chardin. Several decades of paleonto-logical research, carried out mostly in China (and what a lonely task that must have been only he knew), led him to conceive of humanity as a becoming to divine consciousness through time and the destination of its journey a return to its source in God. He also believed that this journey was never without memories of its beginnings.[2,3] This point of resonance with the thinking of Carl Jung, who believed that humankind carries memories of the past in its collective consciousness, brings to mind yet again the coherence of thought by the few who have engaged examination of the evolution of human consciousness.

More recently, in writing about the power of memory and energy and their many manifestations, Rupert Sheldrake suggested that there is an energy that holds the blueprints for species-specific morphology and function whose duties may be compared to that of a monitor which he calls "Morphic Resonance."[4] It has also been described as an entity that somehow, by establishing habits, prompts other memories what to do. If this is so, then, juxtaposing it with genetic and other accompanying energies, it seems reasonable to deduce that if, following conception, they are out of tune with each other during early development, attempts will be made to correct this dissonance in the interest of preserving species specific morphological and functional integrity and purity. That such is, in fact, the case is strongly supported by a unique epidemiological study conducted on the island of Kauai in Hawaii over a period of 20 years commencing in 1955.[5]

Beginning in the prenatal period, the Kauai study followed all the children who survived conception in an entire community representing all socioeconomic and ethnic groups on the island and maintained the cooperation of 90% of them throughout the second decade of their lives. The study addressed many parameters of child development

---

[2] Pierre Teilhard de Chardin, *Human Energy* (New York, NY Harcourt Brace) English Translation (London,UK: William Collins, 1969).

[3] Pierre Teilhard de Chardin, *Building the Earth* [Dimension Books USA 1965]

[4] Rupert Sheldrake, *A New Science of Life.* (Cambridge, UK: Cambridge University Press, 1981); and *The Presence of the Past.* (Cambridge, UK: Cambridge University Press, 1988).

[5] Werner, Bierman and French, *The Children of Kauai*, 1971: Werner and R. Smith, *Kauai's Children Come of Age*, (Hawaii: University of Hawaii Press), 1977.

and the consequences of the threats and stresses that occurred in the perinatal period defined as from 20 weeks of gestation to 28 days of life. Overall, the researchers provided a wealth of information about *why we are the way we are* that seems not to have received the attention it deserves. However, regarding its relation to this polemic, it was reported that of pregnancies reaching 4 week's gestation, an estimated 237 per 1000 ended in loss of the conceptus. The rate of loss formed a decreasing curve from as high as 108/1000 women under observation in the period of 4 to 7 weeks of gestation to a low of 3/1000 in the period of 32 to 35 weeks of gestation. What this indicates is that when, for whatever reason or reasons, genetic *memories* and their energies are damaged in the process of being passed from one generation to another, and therefore cannot jibe, respond, or interact with others and the protective memory of morphic resonance, there are consequences. These range along a linear path of those so severe, resulting in death to the conceptus, which, from this data, would appear to happen in a surprisingly high proportion of pregnancies, to the least severe, allowing intrauterine development to continue to birth but with some injury to morphology and/or function at some stage or even throughout independent life.

The Kauai study sheds light on these later outcomes. The perinatal mortality rate, based on fetal deaths of 20 weeks or more and on infant deaths under 28 days, was 35.9% per 1000 pregnancies. Of the remaining live-born infants, by age two, 3.7% were diagnosed as severely handicapped, requiring long-term medical or custodial care, while 6.3% were diagnosed with conditions requiring short-term medical or nursing care. However, by age 10, 6.6% of the children were deemed moderately or severely handicapped as a result of physical or mental defects or both. Of these, over five times as many children required special educational services (39%) compared to those who required medical care and almost twice as many had emotional and behavioral problems interfering with school progress.

In summation, for an estimated 1311 pregnancies that had advanced to 4 week's gestation, 10 years later only 660 children, that is, half of the pregnancies, were functioning adequately in school and had no *recognized* physical, intellectual, or behavioral problems.

This study and others clearly point to other very important and fundamental issues. First, *memory*, whatever its nature and residence - reaches not only for physical survival but also, more importantly, for physical integrity. The high degree of casualties following fertilization reflects nature's bent to perfection, not so much by not making mistakes but, once made, by seeking to remedy them. This is a theme, if not also a deep knowing, echoed by Henry Skolimowski's imagery in his book "*The Theater of the Mind*," in which he says, "Glory to evolution, for it is God. God is evolution realizing itself, transforming us into more and more radiant fragments of Godliness. We are God in the making. We learn the meaning of God in the process of becoming one. The terror of this realization must not be license for arrogance but an invitation to humility." In so saying he echoes the words of Pierre Teilhard de Chardin, "Some day," he wrote, "we shall harness – for God – the energies of love. And then, for the second time in the history of the world, humankind will have discovered fire."

Second, and closely related to the first, the relatively high percentage of survivors with mental and emotional handicaps clearly documents the early genesis and long-term fallout of injured *memories* that have their impact on the expression of the mind and soul.

Talking of SOUL can be contentious and although in recent years much has been written about it, for the most part it still begs enlightenment on its nature and origins. So elusive is it of easy definition the Oxford Universal Dictionary devotes almost an entire page in attempting to describe it and as with Memory and Consciousness, our Western approach to defining substance by listing its attributes is evident. SOUL is described, among other things, as the seat of feelings and emotion, the feeling and spiritual part of our human nature and the Principle of Life. But, the source of all life is God, and all life is encoded in *memory*. Therefore, SOUL can be perceived as that which is eternal, containing the *memory* of our beginnings in God and which, throughout our lives, seeks living union with its source. Furthermore, if we take its characteristics as reflective of its essence, it is the feeling part of us that connects us to the Sacred of our origins; and, since we share our origins with all of creation, it is also that which connects us with each other. SOUL is therefore, among other things but, primarily, that which gives us a sense of our own unique identity and, within the quality of its early memories, our capacity or otherwise to relate to ourselves and others. If these memories are injured, we will suffer in varying degrees from a diminution or loss of self-identity and the ability to relate soulfully to others.

**This is the context within which I use and define the word SOUL.**

Over the past century or so, certainly since the time of Freud, disturbances of self-identity and the ability to relate to others and reality have been perceived as disorders of thought around which have developed countless theories and therapies of psychology and psychiatry. Perhaps we miss the real meaning of psychology and psychiatry for the root of both words derives from *Psyche* who was the God of the Soul. While it is inevitable that disorders of self-identity and inter-personal relatedness result in disorders of thought, perception, feelings and behavior, the disorders themselves have their origins in *memories*. We now know that the texture of our feelings and, thus, our behavioral tendencies are woven from the fabric of our early sensory and emotional experiences beginning, many scientists believe, in the prenatal period, if not before.

While these early experiences are beyond our conscious recall, the *memories* of them, modified by the *memories* of feelings passed to us in our genes and other energy systems from our parents and their forebears, become the initial locks and keys of how we will "feelingly" respond to life. In other words, they form the bases upon which all other experience will be grafted and interpreted. Likewise, they set the stage for how immune our soul will be to the experiences of life that seek to disconnect us from our true heritage as children of God and of Love. If these initial encounters are loving and welcoming, they will create positive, nurturing memories in the soul, thus creating strong immunization against the effects of all that subsequently seeks to disconnect it from its source and likewise facilitating our ability to relate positively to others. If these encounters are not loving or welcoming, the memories so created provide weak immunization against the assaults that seek to separate the soul from the source of its life in

God, thus, diminishing our ability to relate with others. If not ameliorated by therapy and/or other means and, indeed, if reinforced by later experience, these negative memories lead to feelings of worthlessness, hopelessness, and ultimately to a belief that all that is external to one-self is hostile. Surely, the small step from this to overt violence is clearly evident.

*How all of this plays out in our later life becomes a drama of cosmic proportions because how every individual feels and behaves becomes a part of the collective consciousness that drives world affairs.*

Allow me to introduce the drama by describing in scientific terms the likely long-term effects of our initial sensory encounters. Recent research has found that if a newborn infant is not held skin-to-skin with its mother within six hours of birth, the chemistry of neuro-transmission in the amygdala nucleus located in the limbic system, which is that part of the brain that controls emotion and feeling, changes. The amygdala nucleus modulates levels of aggression through its role as coordinator of sensory input from the neo-cortex, the center for thought. This results in the activation of the hypothalamus which is the part of the brain that controls the autonomic system and, likewise, has direct and controlling connections to the endocrine system, as well as the immune system. Here is where the experiential drama begins. The autonomic nervous system controls every automatic function of the body which is the reason why the energy of feelings is felt throughout the body. Thus, from shortly after birth, our later tendencies to aggressivity or passivity that are derived from feelings, as well as our gut reactions to threat, whether real or perceived, are stamped in the memory banks of our body and soul. These feelings either enhance or cast a shadow over the primal memory of our beginnings in God. This is why it is so essential that all infants particularly those cared for in neonatal intensive care units be touched, held, and stroked in a loving, reas-suring way as often as possible.[6] The intention is to counteract the long-term effects of the somewhat violent nature of the invasive needle and other procedures necessary to save their lives which create memories of

---

[6] Journal of Pediatrics (January 1993).

violent feelings that could then influence later experience. Without this intervention of loving reassuring touch, these infants may become candidates for Reactive Attachment Disorder of Infants and Early Childhood (RADIEC) which results from poor or absent bonding at birth and manifests as emotional and behavioral dysfunction throughout childhood and later life.[7] In addition, other recent observations on emotional development in children indicate that the constancy of loving and nurturing contact with the mother in the first six months of life facilitates the subsequent ability to make and maintain healthy human relationships. Does all this point to the validation of the old axiom, "The hand that rocks the cradle, rules the world?" It certainly seems so and, as such, has a profound message if we have the ears to hear in terms of redressing the soul sickness and violence in our society that has reached epidemic proportion.

Recent data from the U.S. Longitudinal Study on Children and Adolescence suggests that 29% of children between the ages of seven and fourteen have severe emotional, behavioral, and learning disorders, not just any disorder, but a *severe* disorder. Since fear and anxiety result from negative experiences and are inherent components of these disorders, it behooves us to make the connection and to facilitate and encourage mothers, by whatever means, to lovingly nurture their infants and

---

[7]*Reactive Attachment Disorder of Infancy or Early Childhood* (RADIEC): (A) Markedly disturbed social relatedness in most contexts, beginning before the age of five, as evidenced by either [1] or [2]: [1]-persistent failure to initiate or respond to most social interactions (e.g., in infants, absence of visual tracking and reciprocal play, lack of vocal imitation or playfulness, apathy, little or no spontaneity; at later ages, lack of or little curiosity and social interest); [2]-indiscriminate sociability, e.g., excessive familiarity with relative strangers or making requests and displaying affection. (B) The disturbance in A is not a symptom of either Mental Retardation or a Pervasive Developmental Disorder, such as Autistic Disorder. (C) Grossly pathogenic care, as evidenced by at least one of the following: [1]-persistent disregard of the child's basic emotional needs for comfort, stimulation, and affection. Examples: overly harsh punishment by caregiver; consistent neglect by caregiver; [2]-persistent disregard of the child's basic physical needs, including nutrition, adequate housing, and protection from physical danger and assault (including sexual abuse); [3]-repeated change of primary caregiver so that stable attachments are not possible, e.g., frequent changes in foster parents. (D) There is a presumption that the care described in C is responsible for the disturbed behavior in A; this presumption is warranted in the disturbance if A began following the pathogenic care in C. Taken from DSM-III-R (313.89).

children. Since many themselves come to motherhood deprived of positive nurturing, the task is formidable, but not impossible.

*Indeed, as more and more of the secrets of God's creation unfold, motherhood is revealed as the most sacred of vocations and occupations bar none.*

Indeed, if the sacredness of mothering was promoted and fostered, I venture to say that if all other factors were equal, the proclivity to violence in our world would be substantially diminished. Enabling healthy mothering is a priority for world peace

Important as these experiences immediately following birth may be, they are preceded by what happens from conception throughout prenatal life. Many people today are aware of the deleterious and often catastrophic effects on the fetus and newborn child due to the mother's drug use during pregnancy. Some of these effects include premature birth, along with all of the hazards associated with it, including growth retardation, microcephaly, birth defects, and other conditions that seriously jeopardize the quality of life for the child, which of course, has its fallout on all of society. In some jurisdictions throughout the world, drug-using mothers-to-be have been sent to jail for endangering the lives of their infants. When separated from their mothers, this only inflicts more injury on the child. However, what is less well known is how the thoughts, feelings, and moods of the mother impact upon the unborn child. In his book *The Secret World of the Unborn Child*, Thomas Verney vividly describes these reactions, all of which become imprinted in their memory banks.[8]

Leaning on the concepts of holography, which is that the memory of the whole is in even the tiniest part of the whole, Stanislaus Grof, in his book *The Holotropic Mind*, goes a step further.[9] He codified the memories of conception and of intrauterine, as well as perinatal experience into what he terms four Basic Perinatal Matrices, or BPMs. Perinatal is defined, in this context, as

---

[8] Thomas Verney, *The Secret Life of the Unborn Child* (New York, NY Delta Publishing, 1987).
[9] Stanislaus Grof, *The Holotropic Mind* (San Francisco, CA: HarperCollins, 1990).

the time interval between conception and the twenty-eighth day of postnatal life.

The first matrix, BPM-1, which can be called the "amniotic universe," refers to our experiences in the womb prior to the onset of delivery. This means that what happens to the mother in terms of her thoughts, feelings, and behavior become memories within the body, mind, and soul of the yet unborn child.

The second matrix, BPM-2, refers to cosmic engulfment with no exit. It pertains to our experiences when uterine contractions begin but before the cervix opens to liberate us.

The third matrix, BPM-3, refers to the death and rebirth struggles of our lives, and reflects our experiences of moving through the birth canal.

The fourth matrix, BPM-4, is the death and rebirth theme that is related to our experiences when we leave the mother's body.

Dr. Grof claims that each perinatal matrix has its own specific biological, psychological, and spiritual aspects and that they not only incorporate the Archetypes of Jung, but are the *memories* from which we react to the circumstances of our human journey. In my work with children, while breathing quietly during relaxation, they will often, and quite spontaneously, be in touch with the memories of their conception and intrauterine life from which they and I can enter into healing of negative experiences that were associated with it. Enabling children to accomplish this can literally change their lives and how they perceive themselves and the rest of the world, thus laying foundations for becoming healthier and functional adults.

The power of early *memories* is further supported by research about newborn behavior. This indicates that *memory* supports all their cognitive activity such as learning and communication, making their abilities in this regard appear to be innate, i.e., having arrived with them rather than resulting from a progression of development. Making use of such innate talents, newborns demonstrate both *memory* and intelligence as they discriminate novel from familiar stimuli and thus vigorously shape their environment to meet their needs.

These perspectives provide a context of authenticity for the many signs of fetal and birth memory and consequences of birth trauma that have emerged repetitively and been reported by credible observers in professional journals over the past 100 years. Unfortunately they have been largely ignored in terms of their determining role in the aetiology of emotional and behavioral disorders. They also relegate to history many unfounded beliefs about the brain, including the idea that early parts of the brain lie idle until more important parts are developed which is reminiscent of John Locke's dictum that infants wait upon their elders to fill their minds. Likewise, it strongly suggests that the conduction of energy impulses, electrochemical and otherwise, along nerve fibers is certainly not the sole or major means of communication in the nervous system. In fact, memory - and it must be *transgenerational memory* - is at work from the moment of conception, and even before, to equip them to be thinking, feeling and responsive individuals ready to dialogue and even change for the better the adult world - if it were only wise enough to dialogue with them. When we learn to listen, therein will be great hope for the future.

Evidence of the forever-ness of holotropic memory received a spectacular endorsement as a result of the cloning of Dolly, the ewe, in 1997. Once the memories of how to behave as a cell in the mammary gland of the donor ewe were shut off, the genetic blueprints of memories for making the entire animal were set free. Interestingly, this cell had to be implanted into an egg cell from another sheep from which the nucleus had been removed because only the egg cell contains the proteins, and their attendant energies, necessary to turn on the genes and to keep them on their developmental track. Two years after the fact, Dolly is showing signs that she is genetically older than her chronological age; in fact, about the same age as the ewe from which she was cloned, which all goes to show how pervasive are genetic and other *memories*.

Though there is endless more to tell about *memory*, nevertheless, I think it is necessary to briefly mention the controversies presently engulfing what is referred to as "Repressed Memory." It has become a major problem for counselors everywhere and has caused great suffering to those falsely accused of abuse, ostensibly "discovered" during counseling. Responsible counseling demands that clients should essentially be in control of their own journey into healing, with the reassuring and measured guidance of a professional, proficient counselor, much like, but different in its non-directiveness from the free association that is used in psychoanalysis. Since all counseling is a dialogue of sorts between counselor and the one being counseled, repressed memories can emerge in two major ways. First, the client seeks counseling because of dysfunctional feelings and behavior that are making their lives painful, if not intolerable. Memories of feelings of rejection experienced from the moment of conception or birth as well as during infancy and childhood which are often not in their waking consciousness but nevertheless interfering with their lives can, I believe, by an internal process of transference during counseling, be channeled into avenues of recall of physical and/or sexual abuse which may or may not have happened. A climate such as is active presently, wherein abuse of all kinds has high visibility, may serve to heighten the possibility of this happening. It should be borne in mind that the emotional pain and consequences of rejection, which is abuse in and of itself, can be just as serious as those resulting from actual physical or sexual abuse, and of course, memories of actual physical and sexual abuse can also be suppressed and frequently are. Second, a counselor may inadvertently give suggestions to a client as to what may have happened in their past. These may become imprinted in the client's recall as actual happenings in their lives which they are told, due to their painful overtones, have been repressed in their waking consciousness. The effects of these so-called repressed memories are then perceived as the cause of the client's present dysfunction and disability. Since uncovering the cause of suffering, whether it be real or imagined, is relief in itself, it is easy to see how these "repressed but enabled memories" become the focus of the client's pursuit of resolution. In my opinion, until we have a clearer vision of the dynamic inherent in repressed memory and its phenomena, we should not deny its existence as a powerful progenitor of human dysfunction and suffering. However, we should be very cautious about using it at face value in an accusatory way that affects the lives and well being of people the counselee may identify as their persecutors. Until such time, we should call this phenomenon, Enabled Memories.

From all of the foregoing it is clear that *memory* is an exquisite tapestry of many colorful threads; some of which we share with all of humanity, and some which are personal to us. Carl Jung referred to those that are a shared inheritance as the Collective Consciousness, and described them in terms of archetypes. These interact with our own prenatal and perinatal memories, as well as those of our early childhood to become the matrix of the consciousness that drives us in body, mind, and soul and the personalities we thereby become. In seeking the causes of our felt sense of separation from source, which injures our own sense of personal identity, as well as our ability to relate to others, we need to look to the quality of *memories* in our soul. Their profundity is reflected in the story of one American couple's noble attempt to give love to an abused child from Russia. In "Love Isn't always Enough," their anguish is described in the following letter to the editor that appeared in the July 7, 1997 issue of *Newsweek*.

### Love Isn't Always Enough

*My husband and I adopted a 10-year-old girl from Russia with no preparation for the horror to come ("Bringing Kids All the Way Home, "LIFESTYLES, June 16). She came from a severely alcoholic family in which she had to steal food to survive. Her father knifed her, her mother was a prostitute and her brother sexually molested her She lived on the street for a year before going into the orphanage at the age of 9. I received none of this information until she began speaking English and told me herself. The year my daughter lived with us was hell. She was like a wild animal in our home. Eventually, she was diagnosed as being severely disturbed with attachment disorder and aggressive tendencies. We were warned to put alarms on her bedroom door to protect ourselves from her at night. We couldn't live like this. In the most heartbreaking decision I've ever made, we disrupted our adoption. I feel very strongly that agencies need to obtain the same in-depth information about both prospective adoptive children and prospective adoptive parents. To bring a severely disturbed child into an unprepared family sets both the child and the parents up for failure.*

Another letter of equal importance followed this report. This second letter positioned for review the precise dilemma at hand.

*I was disappointed at the softness of Newsweek's piece on international adoption. Contrary to Bethany DeNardo's assertion, that with `stimulation and loving care and good food' the kids can `bounce back' becomes terribly unfair to both adoptive parents and their children. With your research and access to so many scientific studies and facts, you could have enabled readers to begin to understand some of the horrific problems associated with some adoptions of post-institutionalized children. I realize that this tough issue is not easy to look at, but it is an important story that needs to be told.*

**Not until we penetrate and change the negative energies of such powerful, hurtful, and destructive memories will we ever be able to create the positive energies that will nurture and enrich a functional consciousness of self and other.**

# II

## *Weaving Religion and Culture into the Webs of Memory and Consciousness*

But what, you may be inquiring is the connection between what you have just read and "Who and Where is God?"

Well, in so many ways GOD has been hijacked, captured, and imprisoned by religion(s). In a word, GOD has been "made-over" by mankind and this make-over has become an important, if not also a central, part of humanity's history. None of us can escape being influenced and directed by the cultural and religious beliefs of our parents and ancestors, so if we put memory and consciousness into the context of the cultures and religions into which we are born, allegiances to which the majority of humankind carry with them throughout their lives, then, it has EVERYTHING to do with the way we are.

So, let us take a look at how this works.

Religion and culture are closely intertwined and although the boundaries between them are blurred, nevertheless each wields power and control over its constituents in similar ways. They do so by assignments of status to selected individuals and groups, thus conferring authority and privilege on some and withholding it from others. These hierarchies and aristocracies of power direct and monitor beliefs about all manner of subjects, thereby dictating, if not actually controlling the thoughts, feelings, reactions, and behavior of their constituencies. These religious and cultural beliefs and the behavioral responses they evoke have evolved over millennia; They have been, and continue to be, passed as memories of belief and ritual from generation to generation, thus dictating individual and collective behavior at each point in time. As such they are major players in problems that currently divide the world, solutions to which will not be found until we fully understand their origins. Only then will we be able to apply appropriate remedies using and inculcating the themes that are at the heart and center of ALL religions; LOVE, COMPASSION, JUSTICE, EQUALITY, RESPECT for others, and the sister and brotherhoods that flow from our shared heritage as children of the same GOD.

If these be the intent of religion and its high ideals then what took place to dim and change it, leaving religion as a divisive rather than a cohesive force that can bring peace to the hearts and souls of all?

Wisdom cautions that if we do not learn from history we will be bound to repeat it. If this be so then let us take a brief journey backwards into the blood letting of history. What we find is that most wars and other atrocities have been fought over differences of religion and the cultural beliefs and practices they engender. In all instances the scenario is similar. The protagonists believe that the religion they espouse and all that goes with it is the only true religion, thus making all others false and their adherents infidels. Once this belief takes root in the collective consciousness of one group or another, it automatically confers permission to shun, injure, and even kill in the name of GOD and for the sake of GOD those they consider to be blasphemous in their beliefs simply because they are different. In fact, as Elaine Pagels points out in her book, *The Origin of Satan*, the early Christians shamelessly made out their opponents to be the devil.[1] The Crusades of the Middle Ages are an example of the long-term violence and bloodshed that can result from these passionately held and, most often, mindless beliefs. That memories of these experiences and events dwell within the collective consciousness and play a role in collective human behavior cannot be denied. Twentieth century eruptions of ethnic, religious, and internecine wars and the unspeakable brutalities opposing sides inflict on each other confirms it is still a powerful operative in the affairs of humankind.

Yet humankind yearns for this to change.

It takes only a moment of reflection to realize that it is inconceivable that the GOD from whom flows the divine tenets for human behavior in *all religions* could or would take sides in such conflicts, let alone sanction them. But

---

[1] Elaine Pagels, *The Origin of Satan* [Random House: NY, 1995].

alas history is replete with instances where armies arrayed for battle against others because of differences in religious belief have been blessed and spurred on to VICTORY for GOD by their religious leaders. This mind set has also fed missionary zeal and in the many denominations of Christianity, themselves the result of differences in what should be believed and how it should be practiced, has given rise to a numbers game, each faction trying to out do the others in terms of the numbers of converts to their way, as if this itself conferred legitimacy on their way, being THE WAY.

If GOD is truly omnipotent and omnipresent then surely it is unbelievable arrogance to think that GOD needs humans to decide which religion pleases the GODHEAD more and to pontificate which is right and which is wrong. Clearly, what is operative here is the using of GOD as Commander-in-Chief and ultimate authority, to substantiate the ambitions of men who in most echelons of organized religion desire power and control over others, including first and foremost their own followers in all aspects of human behavior, existence, and endeavor. Such control serves only to emphasize conformity to authority rather than the development of personal spirituality which serves to further distance the individual from at-one-ment with their creative source which is what they seek and yearn for.

Furthermore because institutional religions reside within the cultures of their adherents it is inevitable that they feed on each other. Thus when one gravitates to material power, status, and wealth, the other rides in tandem, an alliance that has been, like all others, subject to political and other checks and balances. But the memories of how they have interacted to preserve their common interests of power and control remain within their collective and shared consciousness and continually seek expression, even to this day.

Let me elucidate this phenomenon by briefly tracking it through the Judeo-Christian tradition into which I was born.

All traditions bequeath their gifts as well as their problems, so I start this journey with great respect and gratitude for the wondrous gifts of literature, art, music, poetry, and architecture which it has inspired for over four millennia. Fortunately, the memories of original identity have not only endured, but have been enriched by the hidden and holy lives and activities of monks and nuns in the East and the West, who left us blueprints of how to be in touch with it. In this regard, it is worthy of note that while there have been Church leaders of exemplary character and holiness, relatively few canonized and therefore visible saints of the Christian church have come from their hierarchies. For the most part, they were souls who walked humbly with their God and came from the ranks of the ordinary, but lived extra-ordinary lives. Thus the inspiration and gifts of religion are derived not so much from their organized and legalistic institutions but from those who followed its mystical traditions. Thus it is to the nuns and monks we must give thanks, in particular for perceiving and bequeathing the pure gold of love and tolerance at the center of the dross which is the shared heritage of all religions.[2]

---

[2] After writing this book I came across a document entitled; *Declaration on the Role of Religion in the Promotion of a Culture of Peace*. It echoes the messages of this book. I am including it as an Appendix.

# III

## Original Identity, Original Sin, and Their Legacies

THE BOOK OF GENESIS is regarded as the first book of the Hebrew scriptures, but in fact it was the last to be written and the Hebrew Scriptures themselves are nowadays most frequently referred to as the Old Testament of the Judeo-Christian scriptures.[1] Genesis tells the story of Creation and that on the sixth day God declared, "Let us make man in our image and after our likeness."' God did and was well pleased. So well pleased was God, in fact, that on the seventh day God rested from the labor of creation. Soon thereafter, feeling refreshed and renewed, God took a trip to the Garden of Eden. Herein dwelt all the plants and birds and animals that God had created before He made man and over which He now gave him dominion.

This man apparently wanted for nothing, including the personal attention of God. It was Paradise! But, did he know it? Evidently, not, for when God encountered the man on whom the name Adam had been conferred, much to his surprise He found him unhappy. On questioning him, the man confided that he was lonely. "Hmm," said God, "let me think about this and see what I can do to rectify it." A few days later God visited the man again. Observing that he looked rather tired, God suggested that the man take a nap, which he did. When God saw the energy waves of Stage 4 of the sleep cycle emanating from Adam's head, He performed the quickest transplant in all of medical history. Swiftly opening the man's chest through the smallest of incisions, God removed the twelfth rib on the man's right side, notably the smallest of all he possessed. Then, showering divine energy on it, within an instant God created a companion for the man, and "He" called this new creation, WOMAN,

---

[1] Genesis 1: 26a (New American Bible edition).

SHE who would shortly thereafter become the means whereby all the furies of Hell were said to have been let loose.

Not too long after her debut in the Garden of Eden, Eve, as the woman was now called, began to feel lonesome herself and thought that there must be more to life than just being a companion to Adam. One day, perceiving her discontent, a snake engaged Eve in conversation.

"There is more to life than this you know," the snake said. "You were made for greater things than just being with man."

"Oh, really?" replied Eve. "Tell me more."

"Well," said the snake, "all you have to do is eat the fruit of the Tree of Knowledge and you will become like God, knowing good and evil."

"How can that be?" replied Eve. Do you not know that despite this story of me being just a rib, *I am Wisdom*, and according to the scriptures I, as WISDOM, was before all creation? Besides, God told us not to eat of the fruit of that tree."

"Well, Knowledge is different from Wisdom," replied the snake. "But, putting that aside, don't you think that since you were an afterthought in God's plan for Creation, you should attempt to equalize that by gaining knowledge as well as wisdom? Believe me, if you eat the fruit of that tree, you can gain everlasting fame."

"How so?" asked Eve.

"Well, the story will be told that, because of your disobedience, you are to blame for all the evil that befalls mankind and this will rest on you for ever more."

"Oh!" said Eve. "I'm not sure I believe you but, then, maybe that would be better than being bored. I'll take the fruit!"

Crunching into the apple, she said, "This is delicious! I must share it with Adam." And so, she did. He accepted it willingly and agreed with Eve that it tasted good.

When God learned of what had happened, He made a hasty trip back to the Garden. Hearing Him moving about, Adam and Eve hid themselves in the bushes.

"Where are you?" God called out.

"I am hiding," replied Adam.

"Come here before me," commanded God. Adam did as he was told.

"Why are you hiding? What have you done?" demanded God.

"We ate an apple," said Adam.

"Of which tree," enquired God.

"The tree of knowledge," replied Adam.

"But didn't I forbid you to eat the fruit of that tree," thundered God.

"I believe so," replied Adam.

"Yes or no?" demanded God.

"Hmm. Yes, but Eve made me do it!"

Looking sad, as well as stern, God told Adam to bring the woman to Him because what He had to say applied to both of them. Whereupon, Adam told the woman to leave her hiding place and stand with him before God. Without asking her if what Adam had said was true, God pronounced to them both that, due to their disobedience, they could no longer live in Paradise and that they both must leave the Garden immediately. Furthermore, from henceforward, Woman and her descendents would be associated with the serpent of deception, thereby subject forevermore to Man, who would be the arbiter of the essence, the quality, and the boundaries of her life.

Shortly after being banished from Paradise, and presumably because their new-found knowledge informed them of the possibilities inherent in their nakedness, a condition they supposedly previously had not noticed, they begat two sons, Cain and Abel, who became famous as the poster boys for sibling rivalry and family feuds. Engendered by resentment, jealousy and its resulting blind hatred, Cain murdered his brother Abel, not because of any personal hurt inflicted upon his person, nor of any other wrong doing, but simply because Cain perceived Abel to be God's favorite.

Following the death of Abel, Adam and Eve, the primal parents of Genesis, were left with one son and no daughters - or at least none that are included in the story. Yet, the biblical narrative continues by recounting the names and activities of countless generations that followed. The gullibility that would accept such an improbable story really tests the limits of imagination. Indeed, as a story of how creation occurred, Genesis has long been submerged under the weight of paleontological and other scientific research, which evidence reveals Creation to have been a phenomenon of incredible majesty evolving over several thousands of millennia. But, as a mythic tale of how evil and suffering entered the human domain, as well as how it has remained there pursuing its own trajectory of evolution, Genesis is a masterful backdrop to the human condition.

In pre-Genesis Hebrew culture, the presence of God, the Shekhinah, was referred to in the feminine. In fact, there were a number of gods (Elohim), both male and female, bearing many names. Lilith was "She" who was the creator of life who, herself, had emerged from the great Mother Earth, the begetter of all natural and human life and of all religions and who was and who is both matrix and nurturer. Yet, the rabbinical writers of Genesis chose to ignore Lilith and instead replaced her with Eve whom they portrayed as a seducer and the destroyer of life in its wholesome, creative holiness and oneness with all creation. By excluding Lilith from the picture and replacing her with Eve, they conspired to masculinize God in toto and then promoted Him as the great creator. This led to a belief in the superiority of the male and the inferior status of the female, as well as her offspring, which together permit the use and abuse of women and children. This trespass on the original sacred identity of women and children is at the center of the continuing confusion about the roles expected of men, as well as women and children and the destructive behaviors and misery that flow from it. Emerging from religious texts makes of it a sacrilege.

That such a dramatic change in values and beliefs, and their subsequent long-term residence in the collective consciousness of humankind, could be accomplished by a few (rabbinical) writers is testimony to the power of the written and spoken word. Their monumental betrayal and subversion of what had previously been believed begs the question - WHY? Why did they do this? As in all such similar human situations, fear of that which was being betrayed, accompanied by lust for power and control, were undoubtedly fuel to its fire. In this instance, what was being betrayed was the power of the creative and spiritual feminine which, alas, is still very evident today as it has been throughout the post Genesis Judaic and Christian eras and perhaps deriving from a memory echoing in the male consciousness of the maleness that wrought the change. How it was done is another mystery, maybe, just maybe, a slip of the pen or, more likely as some scholars suggest, a poor choice in subsequent interpretation. The fact that the text can bear constructs equally acceptable scholastically, but which would change its message and meaning, suggests the use of deliberate license with interpretation. But then, of course, it could have been a well-thought-out way of transferring feminine power to the masculine experience; however, over all the theories rests the certainty that barring divine intervention, we shall never know the real reason(s) of why and how.[2] Nevertheless, what took place changed the way much of how humankind had previously perceived itself, which was as people of the land, forest, and sea, intimately related to the Earth, as Mother, and living as an egalitarian, shamanic society whose spirituality was centered on unity and the immanence of God, the Shekhinah; by so doing, it undeniably fractured its wholeness.

Commenting on this perfidy, Judith Plaskow observed that a god who does not include the goddess is an idol made in man's image.[3] Theologian Elizabeth Schussler-Fiorenza cautions that androcentric texts and linguistic constructions must not be mistaken as trustworthy evidence of human culture and religion.[4] This thought is echoed by Bernadette Brooten who has surveyed Jewish and Hellenistic inscriptions and suggests that religious literature composed by men is the product of men's minds and not a simple mirror image of reality.[5] These latter two statements are strong and while one could, by using them, conduct a polemic regarding the nature of reality, nevertheless, within a historical perspective they are probably fair comment.

---

[2] See footnote at end of this chapter.

[3] Judith Plaskow, *The Right Question Is Theological* in *On Being A Jewish Feminist*, S. Heschel (Ed.). (Schocken: New York, 1983)

[4] Elisabeth Schussler-Fiorenza, *In Memory of Her*. (Crossroads: New York, 1983). Reading of her other works is highly recommended by this author.

[5] Bernadette Brooten, *Women Leaders in the Ancient Synagogue*. (Scholars Press: California, 1982).

Adding to the mystery of *why* Genesis was written is its *timing*. Understandably, there is uncertainty about the dates of the writing and compilation of the Hebrew bible. Some scripture scholars place the writing of Genesis after the period of the compilation of the Law and the Prophets, which took place approximately in the early 400s BCE (Before the Common Era). Yet, most of the events the Old Testament describes took place centuries earlier - 1800 BCE for the time of Abraham and from about 900 BCE for David and Solomon. This raises the possibility that Genesis, or parts of it, were afterthoughts, albeit in hindsight, afterthoughts with an agenda whose program of reconditioning and refocusing mind, soul, and behavior into beliefs that are still very much with us.

Further intrigue is added when, as a chronicle of Creation, it is compared with the Creation stories and myths of other religions. In general, it may be said these conceive Creation to be emanations from God who is more often than not regarded as being both male and female. These emanations, which I surmise are currents of eternal creative energy, initially entered and then subsequently re-enter into eternal cycles of integration, dis-integration, and re-integration. There are many cultural variations on this theme, of which in its own way, Genesis is one. It addresses integration as the experience of Adam and Eve in the Garden of Eden and dis-integration as their expulsion from it following their so-called disobedience. For the Jewish people, re-integration awaits the arrival of a Messiah who, it is believed, will end their exodus and re-establish them as God's chosen. How *HE*, and again the emphasis is on the male, will accomplish this is not clear. It is worth noting, however, that it has frequently been suggested that the Judaic salvation or re-integration that is hoped for will not come from another but from within the heart and soul of each individual - much as some latter-day theologians suggest that Christ Jesus understood salvation as God's intimate involvement with human life here and now, rather than being mediated by an-other or hierarchies of various religions who have assumed ownership and control over it and its fruits.

Furthermore in questioning the origins and authorship of scriptures surely a God who created all of humankind should not be expected to play favorites, which then calls into question the idea of a chosen people as well as the source of this belief. Certainly it cannot be denied that it could be a case of the writers of such ideas stating what they want to believe, thereby creating belief systems that profit them and their followers but cause problems with others, whom the chosen are led to believe are outsiders, in this dance of values and favoritism.

What immediately presents itself as an outcome of such beliefs and the power of memory in human consciousness and culture is the continuing conflict between Jews and Arabs, regardless of whether the latter be Christian or Muslim. Both claim Abraham as their founding progenitor, on the one hand legitimately begotten through Sarah, his wife, and on the other, illegitimately begotten through Hagar, his mistress. Surely a scenario played out with prejudice in countless families ever since. In his book *ABRAHAM*, Bruce Feiler delves into the mystique of Abraham whose belief in a single GOD he considers to be one of the greatest contributions of all time to western civilization and its three (3) major religions, Judaism, Christianity, and Islam. Surely in our time when these three (3) religions are playing such a pivotal role in world politics, finding what unites them becomes profoundly important. In this regard and at a practical level the United Kingdom has taken a major step forward, given that its religious constituency is no longer predominately Christian but reflective of many different religions whose factions and differences have caused riots and bloodshed. The Home Secretary in July 2004 formulated legislation that makes it a crime to use these differences to incite hatred and violence.

Christianity refers to the Hebrew bible as the Old Testament and regards its contents as being the forerunner of the New Testament which chronicles the life of Jesus, the Christ, whom Christians accept as the much hoped for Messiah. He it is, who through his life and death, redeems or re-integrates the consequences of the fall from God's grace of Adam and Eve. That event is conceptualized and referred to as the *Original Sin*, whose imprint is said to be on every human being and which in Christianity is said to be washed away by baptism. Original sin as a concept, *per se*, is unique to Christianity and it is often referred to as the sin of our first parents. However, if there were no first parents called Adam and Eve, where does this leave original sin? As a singular event in time and space, it is almost certainly a non happening. Yet, its hold on the human imagination remains, and not without reason, because it is intimately related to original identity and, indeed, is perceived as the reason original identity or ONE-NESS WITH GOD was lost.

As a religious text, Genesis became doctrine, and doctrine is that which must be believed. It is a doctrine that set the stage and thereafter provided the imprimatur for the superiority and dominance of men, from which they assumed authority and control over women and children. Women and children were thereby effectively expelled to the nether regions of subjugation and servitude. Thus was stolen their original and sacred identity as the vessels of creation and fecundity and the seeds of forever future generations.

This was and this remains the Original sin!

It was the sword with which humankind wounded and still wounds itself, a wound that lies open and weeping, awaiting its healing. Alas, it is not the only wound of which Genesis speaks and which, if we match it with human experience through the ages, leads us into an understanding of the consequences of the loss of our original identity. The story tells us that in the Garden of Eden, there was direct contact with God and the consciousness of man and woman was in tune with the consciousness of all creation. It was perfect; it was *in-tegration*; it was *paradise*. There was immunity from all that could destroy it. When paradise was lost, dis-integration followed. As generation followed generation, immunity to that which could injure or destroy unity with self, others, and with all creation was weakened and became vulnerable to these assaults. Thus, over time, the memories of unity and immanence grew dim, but as with all memories, they were never totally lost. These memories speak to us in the depths of our souls; they remain that still small voice that prompts us to reach and to grasp the creative love of our origin which yearns for re-integration with its source.

However, pursuing the Genesis story as it unfolds, it becomes clear that subsequent to the "Fall," re-integration had to be worked at, but alas using the self-same fruit of the tree of knowledge that caused it. Fortunately, we are not limited by knowledge alone for we are also blessed with intu- ition, perception, and other gifts which, together with knowledge, enable us to assess the environments within us and external to us and to interpret what their interplay may or may not mean in relation to one's self and to others. The thoughts and feelings so generated will be a medley of the memories of in-tegration and its loss, which if overall is positive will manifest as functional and, if negative, will manifest as dysfunctional behavior. Intertwined with this are the consequences of the loss of blissful naturalness that yielded to the scramble to cover nakedness, not only of body, but also of mind and soul. The resulting anxiety and inner sense of dis-connectedness then become major constituents in the matrix of the mask we present to others to cover our insecurities and which we use in the struggle for power, control, and supremacy and even just for survival.

Thus, over time, thoughts and feelings have entered into an intimate relationship with perceptions and interpretations which union has served to further cloud the memory of in-tegration and harmony that existed in Paradise. This, in turn, led to the insecurities and uncertainties of dis-integration which generated other memories of how *self* should respond in self-protection and preservation to all that is external and *non-self*.

These alterations and additions have served to change not only individual consciousness, but collective consciousness as well, the how and consequences of which we will now explore.

---

**Footnote:**

It is worthy of note that in regard to inconsistencies in the New Testament Dr. Bart Ehrman points out in his book, *MISQUOTING JESUS, The Story Behind Who Changed the Bible and Why,* Harper Collins 2005, that the texts we use today are not derived from original texts, these having been lost. They are in fact progeny of countless versions copied from copies written by scribes of varying capabilities and intentions. At times when deciphering became a problem they wrote what they thought the text should mean and sometimes added or subtracted from the texts to correlate with their own beliefs. Further readings of Dr. Ehrman's books as well as those of other New Testament scholars reveal that disagreement amongst early Christians about interpretation was the norm. History informs us these disagreements have led to schisms and the numerous denominations that perceive themselves as authentic interpretations of the message of Christ, even to the present day

# IV

## *The Journey of Human Consciousness*

Throughout history, humankind has been fascinated with consciousness, its nature, its power, and its role in the lives of individuals, as well as within and throughout the entire human family. Like love, it is a many splendoured thing. Therefore, to ask "What is consciousness?" is akin to asking "What is love?" or even "What is life itself?" In the past, it was thought to be the same as knowledge. Roger Bacon, who 700 years ago pioneered this notion, claimed that there were two ways of knowing: one by discourse and argument, and the other by experience. He believed that these two ways were complementary, neither being reducible to the other, and that the exercise of one mode simultaneously with the other was incompatible, if not impossible, which, of course, added yet another obstacle in the journey toward *re-integration*. The first mode, that of discourse and argument, is rational, verbal, and sequential thus linear and measurable. The second mode, that of experience which is spatial, diffuse, intuitive and perceptive, is less susceptible to description and certainly evasive to linear description or research.

Applying these modes to the description of consciousness, we have in Western culture, by using science and education, concentrated on the first. Since it is linear and measurable, we have attempted to define consciousness in the objective and measurable terms of its secondary phenomena, expressed in behavior and verbalization. Thus, it is no surprise that those who have attempted to explain and describe consciousness have come predominantly from our various scientific and educational communities. The second intuitive spatial mode has until recently been largely but not completely ignored in Western culture, but for millennia, has been the norm of inquiry for those of Eastern cultures. This approach to knowing and consciousness places emphasis on personal, subjective, and empirical phenomena that lead to an inner awareness of oneness and connectedness with God and all creation.

Thus, it is no surprise that those who have described it, and continue to do so, come mainly from the monastic traditions of the religions into which they were born, the several paths of Buddhism, the eclecticism of Hinduism, the Tao's of Taoist Chinese philosophy, and also the mystical traditions of Christianity and Islam.

The yearnings of the human soul to know and to be touched by the true meaning of its existence, which is union with God, has, throughout history, evoked a search for a bridge between these polar opposite approaches to elucidating consciousness and knowing, particularly as this applies to human wholeness and holiness. The rapprochement began with religious scholars and writers from both East and West. However, in recent years it has found unlikely allies in Western neuro-physiological research and the imploding field of trans-personal psychology. Both have demonstrated how, in our living and in how we live, i.e., our feelings and behavior, we are bound by the beliefs and concepts that we hold in our minds. As already described these derive in large measure from the memories of our experience: genetic, evolutionary, and personal, as well as the conditioning and the teaching and training we have received.

Several great minds of the 20th century have applied their skills to describing the phenomena associated with consciousness, if not also attempting to define it. The many writings of Pierre Teilhard de Chardin reveal that he conceived of consciousness as a circular journey of energy proceeding from its source, the Alpha Point, through four levels of reality - Matter, Life, Thought, and Spirit - which ultimately over millennia of time will return to its source, the Omega Point, mission accomplished.[1] This concept, applying as it does to collective consciousness follows closely the themes of creation in many religions, namely, Integration, Dis-integration and Re-integration; but his concept may also be perceived as the movement and development of consciousness throughout a person's lifetime. Aldous Huxley also described four levels - Physical, Biological, Psychosocial, and Spiritual[2] - and Abraham Maslow did likewise, but within a more

---

[1] Teilhard de Chardin, *The Phenomenon of Man.* (Mentor Books: New York, 1961).
[2] Aldous Huxley, *Evolution in Action.* (Mentor Books: New York, 1953)

specifically psychological hubris - Behavioristic, Psychoanalytic, Humanistic and Transpersonal.[3] All too much to go into here, but what is interesting is that scientists who have engaged in pursuing the nature of consciousness have not been hesitant in emphasizing its spiritual dimensions. For example, Fritzof Capra the physicist believes that a true science of consciousness will deal with qualities rather than quantities and will be based on shared experiences, and that *soul, feelings,* and *compassion* are its very essence.[4] Neuroscientist Karl Pribram and physicist David Bohm have proposed theories that in tandem appear to account for all transcendental experience, paranormal events, and much else besides.[5,6] As such, they place consciousness within a holotropic frame which since holography embraces all parts of the whole, as well as the past, present, and future, seems logical. His holiness The Dalai Lama echoed these views in a conversation he had with Dr. Wayne Teasdale, of the World Parliament of Religions, in September 1997, he is quoted as saying: "Consciousness involves absolute, non-dual awareness, unified and not primarily human. This consciousness is animated by an infinitely wise compassion. It is very profound and must bear fruit in some kind of service." His comments assure us that science and spirituality can no longer be considered to be mutually exclusive, but are in fact dynamically compatible.

Several other scholars have also expanded the parameters of our understanding; but to simplify what at first may seem to be a maze of opinions, let me here describe Consciousness from two major perspectives: Personal, Individual Consciousness and Evolutionary Consciousness.

The latter, like the collective consciousness of *memory,* to which it is a close relative, evolved as a shared property with all humanity and will be described later. But first, turning attention to individual consciousness, it is

---

[3] Abraham Maslow, *Toward a Humanistic Biology.* American Psychologist 24, 724-735.

[4] Fritzof Capra, *The Turning Point: Science and Society and the Rising of Culture.* (Bantam Books: New York, 1982).

[5] K H. Pribram, *What the Fuss Is About In K Wilber's The Holotropic Paradigm and Otber Paradoxes.* (Shambhala: Boulder, CO, 1982)

[6] D. Bohm, *Wholeness and The Implicate Order.* (Routledge and Paul Kegan: London, 1980).

said to consist of four states: "Waking, Dream, Sleep, and Transcendental." Only in "Waking" consciousness are we aware of our thoughts. Yet, if we have learned anything at all from the great scholars and psychotherapists of this and other centuries, we have to be aware of the profound influence of "dream," "sleep," and "transcendental" consciousness on how we perceive reality and, thus, on how we live our lives. In order to understand why, we need to look at how memories and their energies work together to bring it about. For ease of understanding, it may be compared with the development of a child.

During fetal life and infancy a child is more or less totally dependent on others and is at one with the texture and quality of its environment and sometimes also at its mercy. As a child grows, this dependency lessens as the central nervous and other systems mature, allowing new skills and new awarenesses to be acquired. This leads to new interactive phenomena with the child's environment, giving new meaning to life and existence at each stage of development. Abundant research, including that which I have quoted in this and other of my writings, shows beyond doubt that the nature and quality of these interactive phenomena convey messages and create expectations about the world outside of *self* which greatly influence later affect and behavior. In other words, during growth and development, while thoughts and *waking consciousness* change, all experience is stored in the memory banks of body, mind, and soul. These memories, though they can be modified, become the bases of belief systems in terms of inter-personal relationships and thus also of behavior. These experiences likewise have a profound effect, if not also a tutoring role, on ego development. This is at the core of how a child perceives him/herself as a separate, independent human being in relation to others. The urge to be free of parental and/or societal regulation and restriction and to exert one's ego independently reaches its peak during adolescence. If the tutoring of experience has been nurturing, then more than likely the turbulent passage of adolescence will give way sooner rather than later, to relative calm. If however, tutoring has been harsh, punishing, and insensitive, the ego is much more likely to take on the combativeness associated with low self-esteem. This can and frequently does lead into the whole spectrum of self-destructive behavior, including addictions as well as dysfunctional, interpersonal behavior, which latter is direct-ed against a world perceived as hostile to self. It is of course when these impasses occur, whether in children, adolescents, or adults, that we invite professional counseling to liberate those suffering from their emotional and behavioral prisons.[7] Here it is well to state that:

*The purpose of professional counseling is, and should always be, to enable the client to grow into new and healthier awarenesses of self and other This not only permits healing of scars on the soul, but also allows tolerance, love, and compassion to take up a felt residence in their lives.*

But, the trajectory of the development of *individual* consciousness is not only beholden to personal experience. It travels with and is influenced by the consciousness that has evolved over millennia from the memories of shared human experience, labeled by Carl Jung as the "Collective Unconscious."

The subject of debate in East and West about its role in dreams and their meaning, as well as in human aspirations and behavior, it has also played a major role in analyses of the myths that not only envelop our origins but which continue to influence our personal as well as our inter-dependent communal journeys. The world of literature is full of these marvelous messages. Thanks to their popularization in a television series conducted by Bill Moyers of the Public Broadcasting Network in the USA, the writings of Joseph Campbell - particularly his book *"The Hero With a Thousand Faces"* - caught the attention and engaged the imagination of many people worldwide.[8]

Additionally, there have been other scholars and visionaries within, if I may coin an appellation, a psycho-scientific ambiance, who have rendered a teleological understanding of collective consciousness from its begin-nings. Pioneered in the 20th century by scientists such as Robert Ornstein, Dr. David Bohm, and spiritual scholars

---

[7] For additional reading on this subject matter see, Ursula M. Anderson:
   *The Psalms of Children: Their Songs and Laments. Understanding and Healing the Scars on the Souls of Children,* She Bear Publications 1997.
   *Immunology of the Soul: The Paradigm For the Future,* In-Sync Press 2000.
   Taking Out the Violence, Shedding Light on the Science and Soul of Human Behavior, Book Guild, U.K. 2003.
[8] Bill Moyers' Documentary, P.B.S. Television, USA 1993.

such as Fr. Bede Griffiths, nevertheless, I will here briefly outline the hypothesis of Ken Wilber who describes the evolution of consciousness in six stages, always, it seems to me, from its primal source in God which I call eternal energy and in the developmental terms that resonate with human development from conception through adulthood which has just been briefly described. From Stage 1, wherein all creation is at one with its creator, humanity journeys its shared and universal consciousness through the phenomena consequent to its separation from its origin in Creation and creative love to its end or at-one-ment with its primal source. Stage 2 relates to the sense of separation humankind experienced when this one-ness was lost, as it was when Adam and Eve were expelled from the Garden of Eden, and the fears that accompanied the transition from an existence of loving dependency to one wherein this was not palpably present. Language developed in Stage 3, thus allowing description of what was exterior to self by the use of verbal symbols. Language combined with the inner sense of separation from the source of dependent lovingness, which emerged in Stage 2, allowed the concept of blame to form. This was aggrandized during Stage 4 in which ego emerged as a driving force. It also coincided with the rapid development of the neo-cortex in the human brain whose function, among others, is rational and logical thought and their opposites. This not only created within the individual a sense of separate, independent existence, but also provided the means to rationalize and thus intensify the sense of separation of *self from others*. It is within this frame of reference that humankind can create excuses to insist on its individual autonomy and render violence in thought, word and deed on others whom, by being different, it perceives as threats. Stage 5 signals a return to source and, thus, glimmers of an end to the terrors of being separated from it. It is referred to as Trans-Personal consciousness, the awareness that we can reach beyond ourselves to encounter *other* with love and compassion. This hoped for quality for all humanity has always been at the core of personal spiritual experience as well as the written and codified intents of all religions. However, for the past several years, this quality has found a home in the tenets of Trans-Personal Psychology, and with its opening to other, is the prelude to the return to source, bringing consciousness full circle to its beginnings which occurs in

Stage 6. Wilber calls this the stage of supreme consciousness, wherein, through meditation and compassion for others, we can experience God. It is in this stage that we also encounter the meaning of angels and saints as messengers of love and of eternal universal energy."[9] It is believed that we carry within us memories of, and the potential to experience all these levels of consciousness. Stages 1 through 4 are mostly experienced within our dream and sleep consciousness from where they influence our waking consciousness. It is Stage 5 that truly calls us to the journey of being divinely human, the transcendence of self to the realization that *other is also I* and that together we can reach at-one-ment with God.

If we pay attention to the nuances in Wilber's description of the circular motion of the energies within the evolution of consciousness, it resonates in a profound way with the Genesis story of Creation. Wilber's Stage 1 corresponds with integration, the oneness of humankind in harmony with Creation, which is paradise, the Garden of Eden. His Stage 2 reflects the onset of dis-integration, a felt or soulful sense of disorder and disconnectedness from the source of creation, that occurred after the Fall, and the beginning of exile.

Stage 3, wherein language developed, can be equated with the scriptural Tower of Babel. It presaged a growing inability to communicate peacefully, giving rise to enmities, misunderstandings, and consequently many genetic and behavioral adaptations to the ensuing stress. Stage 4 represents the emergence of humankind from the bonding that was family and tribal life lived in natural surroundings to the autonomy of the individual and the growing dominance of ego, a stage that persists to this day. Despite many appearances to the contrary it may be that stage 4 is nearing its apogee. This hoped for reality is reflected in the many signs that we may be at the dawn of Stage 5, such as the concern of stranger for stranger in their extremity as exemplified by those who risk their lives to bring help of all kinds to those suffering because of war, famine, and natural disasters in all parts of the world. More recently, the growing awareness that we are more than the machine that is our body, that we are trinities of body,

---

[9] Wilber in B. Griffith's, *A New Vision of Reality.* (Templegate Publishers: Chicago, Illinois, 1990)

mind, and soul, is entering into general acceptance and even making dents in the ranks of physicians and health-care professionals. Likewise, the increasing use of alternative methods of healing, attempts at rapprochement between religions, and most importantly the awakening to spiritual values rather than the former bondage to organized religion and its hierarchy of control add to these hopeful expectations. Stage 6 corresponds to De Chardin's Omega Point wherein ONE-NESS with Creation is a felt reality.

*What is very interesting when one compares the becoming of Personal Consciousness with Collective Consciousness are the parallels between the two. Surely another example of Holotrophic Memory; what is within the WHOLE resides also within its tiniest particle or fragment or single component.*

These currents plus the high profile emergence of MEDITATION as a means for deep spiritual experience and inner peace has prompted research on the neurology of spiritual experience. Andrew Newberg and Eugene D'Aquhi, two medical doctors studied the brains of Tibetan Buddhist meditators and Franciscan Catholic nuns. They found that the events the meditators considered spiritual were indeed associated with observable neurological activity. The research was based upon the fact that increased blood flow to a given part of the brain correlates with heightened activity in that particular area, and vice versa. For the measurements they used a high-tech brain imaging tool, the SPECT camera (single photon emission computed tomography). At the transcendent peak of the spiritual state, the subject tugged on a string. Radioactive dye was released into an intravenous catheter in their arm and SPECT images of their brain were recorded.[10]

They found that during spiritual activities the frontal lobes of the brain became more active. These areas reflect focused attention and concentration, and are considered the neurological seat of the will. In addition, the spiritual state produced sharp reduction in the activity level of the posterior superior parietal lobe, or "orientation association area" (OAA). One job of the OAA is to draw sharp

[10] A. Newberg, E. D'Aquili and V. Rause, *Why God Won't Go Away: Brain Science and the Biology of Belief*, NY: Ballantine Books, 2002.

distinction between you and everything else; between you and not-you. The second job is to give one the ability to experience a "three dimensional body" and to orient that body in physical space.

The OAA is an area of the brain that never rests. It requires a constant stream of sensory information to do its job well. So what would be the effect to our perception of reality when the OAA is deprived of sensory input as when a person enters a deep spiritual state? The perception of discrete objects would cease, there would be no sense of space or the passage of time, no line between the self and the rest of the universe. In fact, there would be no subjective self at all; there would only be an absolute sense of unity without thought, without words, and without sensation. The mind would exist without ego in a state of pure, undifferentiated awareness. Such unitary states are the transcendent goal of all spiritual paths! Unitary states range from the mildest to the most profound, and represent a span of continuum depending upon the degree that the sensory input to the OAA is blocked. In addition to meditation and prayer such spiritual states can begin with physical activity – any repetitive rhythmic behavior causes the orientation area to be blocked from neural flow. Of course, the process can be set in motion by nothing more tangible than the mind willing itself toward God.

While the SPECT imaging research doesn't prove the existence of God or the Absolute, it does indicate that these spiritual states are as real as any other brain states. Thus, mystical experiences are biologically and scientifically real, and play an evolutionary role in our survival. The great mystics and religious leaders of the past regardless of creed were all attempting to grasp this ungraspable Absolute as are so many ordinary folk of today.[11]

During the millennia it took for human consciousness to evolve through its stages to the present time, there was but one constant and it was *change*. This not only involved how people lived and secured their basic necessities of food, clothing, and shelter, but also how they adapted to their environment which included their reactions to the threats and presence of danger and disease, as well

---

[11] William C. Gough, Foundation for Mind Being Research Newsletter. April 2004.

as how they perceived and related to each other at all levels. Ultimately, of course, these changes involved the genes whose memories of form and function were thereby modified and altered so to ensure survival of the race. Their ability to adapt or, as geneticists would say, mutate, has been highly successful, particularly regarding physical integrity and resilience, as evidenced by the multiplication of the human race in numbers so overwhelming that it almost defies human imagination. Into this equation one must also factor the considerable assists that the genetic memories for physical form, function, and survival received from advances in science, and even much more so, from improvement in the public health and welfare.

But if we look at the changes that more directly influence the quality and functions of soul and its expression in feelings, together with their antecedent thoughts and subsequent behaviors and their impact on consciousness, it is apparent they have *not* enjoyed the same measure of success. Although the caring soul of humanity sometimes blinds us with its light, and despite the good that abounds, nevertheless our world is full of contentions and divisions. Supremacy of ego and distrust of *other* reflects pervasive and worldwide persistence of the genetic memories and other energies that foster these attitudes and behaviors and their fallout transgenerationally. Part of the reason is that health of soul has not received the same intense attention as has health of body. The extent of soul sickness is all too evident in the statistics and stories of violence everywhere, particularly the disturbing increase in violence and abuse done to children *as well as committed by them.* Nevertheless *soul* remains that still small voice within each and all of us that whispers and sometimes shouts about its original identity and its yearning to reclaim and proclaim it.

Because our earthly lives are but a blink on the screen of creation, we may with our blinkered vision be tempted to be discouraged and to think that we are not moving on and towards our source but are stuck at a point of no return. After all, history seeks to tell us that despite all the advances in science and technology, our *collective* behavior as humans seems to have resisted significant change in terms of improvement, but this maybe more apparent than real. In addition, the spiritual teachers who came to remind us of the way to live still await the most of us to listen and to hear. But the evolution of consciousness has been, and remains a long, a very long journey.

However, given the power of memory and consciousness, it is evident that

*"until our beliefs about whom we are as spiritual beings, dependent on each other takes up residence in our souls and in our consciousness, our behavior will not change;*

*BUT IT IS HAPPENING, "*

And there is encouragement.


"The evolution of (wo)man is a gradual ascent through different forms of consciousness to the divine consciousness, which is the ultimate goal of the evolutionary process," said Dom Bede Griffiths, one of the great spiritual leaders of the 20th century, to which I add: this ascent, to be fruitful must be both personal and collective. [12]

Understanding the barriers that impede its blossoming are the gates that we now must open to its unfolding. Prominent amongst these are the memories and attitudes that permit abuse and use of others on the false premise that it comes from authority both cultural and religious. As co-creators of the earth, and pilgrims in the journey of human consciousness back to its source, every woman, child, and man are equal partners regardless of color, race, or creed. Therefore, no one individual or type of person has the primal right of superiority over others. Yet, as a result of the concepts put forward in religious texts, this is precisely what has happened. So, let us now enter the labyrinths of discovery of what the theft of original identity of women and children has wrought.

---

[12] Bede Griffiths, *Vedanta and Christian Faith.* (Templegate Publishers, Chicago, Illinois, 1991).

# V

# *The Consciousness of Woman, Its Historical Roots*

Over the past many years, many women have come to talk with me as therapist or friend or both. To my question, "What seems to be the problem?" the answer I receive is usually a variant of "I don't know whom I am." This applies to women of varying circumstances and positions: women of all races; women who are homemakers; women who are both professionals and homemakers; those who are married and those who are not; those who are rich and those who are poor; as well as the vast in-between we refer to as the middle class. They cry that they have nothing or want more. Ask most of them to tell you what it is that they are missing or what it is they want more of and the answer will almost always be, "I don't know, but somehow I feel empty"

What they are missing is that sense of *self and self-identity* from which flows the dearest of all human gifts, the capacity to be intimate and comfortable with one's self. We tend to think of intimacy as being with another person, but we cannot experience true intimacy with another unless we are first in comfortable intimacy with our own self. Attaining such a state requires effort and discipline. In general, it may be said that loss of original and sacred identity blurs the felt sense of connectedness to our source in creative love to a point where most of us live behind a mask, woven from memories some hidden deep within our consciousness and some deriving from our own experiences.

For the past several millennia, all religions and cultures have promoted and acted on the belief of the supremacy of the male and the subservience and inferiority of the female. It is so pervasive that even at the dawn of the 21st century feminine independence, ability, and curiosity that invokes disobedience to male injunctions or even just expressing opinions leads to all kinds of trouble, resulting not only in injury to the feminine spirit but also quite frequently to verbal and emotional abuse and when physical can lead to her death. Over time, and by virtue of genetic and cultural memories within the collective consciousness, women have been conditioned by the power of this cultural/socio/religious history to the point where they continue to give their inherent power away to men. So it is little wonder that many women say "I don't know who I am," because they not only feel trapped but are trapped behind the masks that permit survival in the culture that puts them down.

Myths and fairy tales from the past tell us about these things. Of such is the story of Bluebeard. Three sisters and their mother were all quite suspicious of him because of his unusual behavior and his very blue beard and they assumed he was very rich because he lived in a castle. However, when he invited them to go to the woods for a picnic, they camouflaged their fears and went with him. It was the youngest sister who persuaded herself that a man who could be so charming and nice could not be bad. Thus, when he asked her to marry him, she agreed. One day, shortly after the wedding, Bluebeard informed his wife that he had to go away. He gave her the keys to everything within the castle, including the key to the one room that he forbade her to enter alone. Well, not surprisingly, curiosity got the better of her and one day she put the key into the lock of the forbidden room. As she did so, the lock began to bleed. In spite of this warning, she continued to insert the key into the lock and then turned it. As she entered the room, to her horror she beheld the remains of previous wives whose curiosity had also gotten the better of them and who, because of their disobedience to the command of the male, were permanently dispossessed of their identities and their lives by none other than their husband and now hers - Bluebeard.

The important part of the story is the bleeding of the lock. It is a metaphor for the consciousness of woman who knows in her soul that by yielding her being and her integrity to male commands *when the intention is control over her*, woman surrenders the sacredness of whom she is. In this story, her brothers rescue the young bride from the killing wrath of Bluebeard just in time, but the damage was already done. Forever now, she, *woman*, will know fear in her relationship with the male, who has shown her the consequences of disobedience to him. Her curiosity, likewise her love for life, has been replaced by a sense of powerlessness. In this story, we see the shadow of Yahweh, the vengeful God in the saga of Adam and Eve.

In the Greek mythology of the pre-Christian era, as well as in Eastern mythology and religions, we glimpse different perspectives on the nature, substance, and role of the feminine. In the story of Demeter and Persephone, we learn of the yearning of Hades, the male god of the underworld, for the beauty, lovingness, and creativity of Persephone. He realizes that to be whole he needs her, and thus when she is out in the fields one day with her mother Demeter, he steals her. The earth goes into mourning and grieves through fall and winter. During this time, Demeter frantically seeks out her daughter and eventually asks the Sun God to help her find Persephone. He tells Demeter that her daughter is in the underworld, to which Demeter hastens in an attempt to rescue her. The Gods tell Hades that if Persephone has not eaten any of the fruits of the underworld, she must be returned to her mother. Grieving over her kidnapping and separation from her mother, Persephone has not eaten, but given the idea by other gods, Hades contrives to have a pomegranate pressed to her lips. As she awakens during the journey back to earth, Persephone moistens her lips with her tongue and ingests some of the juice and a seed from the pomegranate. After doing so, Hades tells the gods that she has indeed eaten some of the fruit of the underworld. The gods then decree that Persephone will now have to spend six months in Hades and six months with her mother on Earth. During her absence, life on earth will go into abeyance, as in fall and winter. However, when she returns, bringing joy with her, spring will move in, seeds will be planted, and the harvest gathered in the summer's heat.

There is a puzzling dichotomy in these stories. In Bluebeard, we are told that unless women obey the male, death will ensue; in other words, women live by permission of the male and on his terms. In the story of Demeter and Persephone, we learn how the male is cold and lifeless without the female and the feminine. Does this confusion and the dilemma it poses sound familiar to those of us living at the dawn of the 21st century? I would say yes, to the utmost degree - and, dilemmas always cause stress.

But, is this all? I fear not!

Let us look now at some of the myths that inform us of how women regard other women in cultures where they are subservient, and what this can do to their sense of self and its consequences. On the surface, the Cinderella story is charming. Yet, if we take a closer look, it is the story of how women often connive to take away the fulfillment and happiness of other women. In most stories about women and their relationships with each other, happiness and fulfillment are equated not with their own personal growth emotionally and spiritually that yields a strong sense of their own idendity, but with what women have been conditioned to believe is the ultimate prize, which is to have a Prince Charming all of one's own. The message is clear: Woman gains identity only by being connected to a man which, if he is indeed Prince Charming, also has power and wealth. In order to gain her prince, Cinderella not only had to deal with the tactics of her jealous step-sisters who were hell bent on preventing her from gaining him, but she also had to run an obstacle course of having things fit just right to make herself worthy of his attention. The plethora of 20th century advertisements, mostly coming from the business world informing women of how they can improve on what nature gave them, leaves no doubt that women are still conditioned to believe they must work at improving themselves in order to be worthy of the male and his attention. But, when they involve themselves with this, do they win? And, how does it sit with other women?

Another story gives insight to the answer. I vividly remember seeing the film *Red Shoes* based on the story of the same name when I was a very young child. Moira Shearer, a beautiful ballerina who was the only rival to Margot Fonteyn in the world of the "Royal Ballet" in England at that time, was the star. Readers, you know the story I am sure, about the little shoeless orphan who gathered rags of all colors and made herself shoes putting the red rags uppermost for the world to see. She exulted in the shoes and loved them because they were a gift of her own creation. One day wandering down a country lane gathering berries, fruits, and nuts to sustain herself, a gilded carriage drew along side and the woman inside leaned out and invited her to get in and go home with her, telling her she would never have to fend for herself again. Once home the first order of business of this woman, who no doubt was well intentioned, was to replace the red shoes that the little girl had made for herself with other red shoes made by a master cobbler. At first, she admired her new shoes enormously, turning them this way and that, but the more she wore these shoes made by another, the less she could control their activity and the more she moved her feet in them, the less she could control their movement. Realizing that she was in great trouble, she tried more than once to get them off and could not because they twirled, and twirled, and twirled and eventually they twirled her into the forest where there lived an executioner. She begged him to remove her new shoes with his axe, but because they and her feet were now, as it were, glued together, he could not do so without cutting off her feet, to which in her desperation she agreed. Thus she became crippled and had to live the rest of her life dependent on others. The message is loud and clear. Her own creativity and her own power were stolen by another woman who thought she knew what was best for her, thus forever taking away her ability to truly become her own creation - *her own self.*

Yet, looking once again at how Woman is regarded in Greek mythology and Eastern religions, we discover that it is Woman, the feminine, who lives in the hidden place that everyone, man and woman, is aware of, yet few have seen or touched. It is the feminine who can show us what is right for the soul; and the *Book of Wisdom* of the Old Testament, written in the feminine says it well.

I *Wisdom* was before all creation.

*She is the eternal intuition, the connection with the eternal and with the creator.*

Indeed, one of the most widespread archetypical personifications in all cultures is that of the wise old woman, the Crone. She it is, who is the feed to the root of an entire instinctual system of yearning and intuition. There are many names for her, including, the heroine/ warrior, the great father/mother and the one who knows. And yet, in religions and cultures of today and their centuries long traditions, she is absent.

Whatever happened to her?

Although she still lives in Memory and Consciousness, is what happened to her as the result of religious and cultural beliefs at the root of woman's sense of loss and self identity?

I believe so.

The great privilege of life and living is becoming and being whom we are and whom we were born to be. It is the endless search for the Holy Grail, the part that is missing that if found will make us whole. There is endless mythology around the Holy Grail, many people still believing that it is the chalice used by Christ at the Last Supper. Other scholars believe that it is the platter on which Christ laid the bread he later broke and gave to his apostles at the Last Supper. History has it that Joseph of Aramethia, who provided the tomb for Jesus Christ, brought the platter to Glastonbury in England, which is the center of the legends that surround the Holy Grail, King Arthur, The Round Table, Queen Guinevere, Sir Lancelot, and Merlin. In the Judeo-Christian tradition, bread and wine are at the symbolic center of worship and represent the nourishment of Life by Eternal Energy, the Great and Holy Spirit, the one GOD. Thus, those who seek the Holy Grail are seeking not the chalice that held the wine or the platter on which the bread was laid, but the Bread and Wine of Life itself, which is to know within our own beings wholeness, love, hope, and oneness with Creation and to be without fear. So if women have had their power to pursue the grail within their own lives stolen from them by men, and blemished by women who resent women who have taken the road to self empowerment, then:

*Whom are we as women?*

*What do we seek?*

*What are the consequences of our agony?*

*Who and what is the FEMININE?"*

# VI

## *The Trinitarian Nature of Woman*

Across all major religions, there is Trinity, including the shared trinity of Integration, Dis-Integration, and Re-Integration. Woman, too, is a trinity. She is first the birther; secondly, the nurturer; thirdly, she is the crone, the wise older woman, the one who knows, who intuits, and who loves unconditionally. The threads that bind this trinity live within Consciousness and Memory.

From about 7000 BCE, people of Southern Europe were agriculturists, matriarchal, and goddess worshipping, taking from the earth what was needed for life and returning with reverence what was no longer needed. As villages were built, many shrines to the goddess were also built. Goddess and woman, giving birth, nurturing, and strengthening their creations was the pivot of their lives. Those who blessed the mother/goddess gathered at sacred wells and springs, some of which continue to exist today, and are becoming increasingly popular as places of historical interest and pilgrimage. Those villages that have been excavated show no signs of weaponry and no signs of animal slaughter. In these ancient burial places, there are many representations of the goddess, "mother of all," with wide hips for birthing and many breasts to nourish symbolically all of earth's children. Women, the embodiment of the goddess, seem to have been treated with great honor and respect.

If we allow ourselves a swift journey from that point in history until now, one must ask, "What have we allowed to be done to our roles, as Woman, giving birth, nurturing, and strengthening our creations as well as using our wisdom to nurture and strengthen Mother Earth?" To find the answers let us look at each of these roles separately.

## Woman As Birther

Most thoughtful people, and in increasing numbers, believe that experiences in the womb and surrounding birth are the most important of every individual's life. They set the stage and create the infrastructure for all subsequent behavior to the end of life. Yet in our society this is given little or no attention, and our way of birthing works against it. For example, about a half-century ago, bureaucratic decisions were made to build large maternity hospitals because hospital births were believed to be the safest. Subsequently, it was assumed, *incorrectly*, that hospital delivery was responsible for the lowering of maternal and infant mortality rates. However, if one examines the trends of maternal infant, and child mortality rates over the last 100 years in most developed nations, it is obvious that the lowering of the mortality rates coincided with implementation of universal education, improved social conditions, the provision of clean water and effective sanitation which resulted in improved health for the public. While no one can argue with the aim of having all women delivered of healthy infants, we should be looking for ways that will also enhance the bonding of mother, infant, and family.

The dilemma resulting from current attitudes and practice has been succinctly addressed by Carmel Duffy, a well known Irish archaeologist. Writing in the August 1991 issue of *Aisling*, a journal published in Ireland, she observed that today childbirth *is a managed affair*. She states, however, that if a woman is to give birth, she must open up absolutely, physically, mentally and spiritually, and let go, so that the new life can come into being. If held on to and managed, the deep spiritual meaning of the experience is hobbled. She further states that during each of her seven pregnancies, she was coerced by her physicians not to have her child delivered at home, but to have it delivered in the hospital. She states that her failure to comply led physicians to intimidate and frighten her into doing things their way. I believe, as she does, that women should not be co-erced, but assisted and encouraged to experience and exercise the power that the Great Spirit of Life has entrusted to them by making them mothers. In this context, I also believe that each woman should ask the meaning of all procedures that are currently carried out during pregnancy. A recent study, for example, showed that sonograms do not improve the immediate outcome of pregnancy. Apart from the expense of these procedures and data that indicates they are doing nothing to improve the immediate outcome of pregnancy, one must ask, what are they doing in the long term to unborn children. Years ago, I suspected that ultrasonography, which at that time, and I believe still is considered by some to be a noninvasive procedure, is actually a highly invasive procedure. The high-frequency waves that go through a woman's body in order to give an image of the fetus are like so many fine-tuned ultra-sharp knives which produce images when they impact on masses of different density, in this case the fetus. Sonograms are routinely done during pregnancy at the time of migration of nerve cells from the notochord to the brain. What is this invasion of high-frequency waves doing to the orderly migration of nerve cells from the notochord, the primitive nervous system, to their intended and appropriately matched nerve fiber locations in the developing brain? I believe it may be scrambling it. Then the obvious question becomes does this have any relation to the rising epidemic of learning and behavioral problems in children? If so, could it be contributing to the pandemic of violence in our society? I think these are questions of profound societal impact and importance, and research should be developed immediately to give us the answers. Also, at about 28 weeks of pregnancy, women are given the glucola test, which is a test to discover whether or not they are at risk for pregnancy induced diabetes. For several hours after the mother has taken the glucola, a fetal heart will frequently beat so fast it is uncountable. Further, what is this doing to sensitize the whole endocrine system of the unborn child to future sugar imbalances, and what is this doing to create memories in the brain for the rush of sugar from drugs and alcohol, a crucial question because electrochemical messages in the cells of our bodies leave memories that remain there for always? Clues to the answer comes from addicts themselves who tell us that what they are addicted to is the memory and pleasure of the rush that their addiction gives them.

Combining all of this with the importance of loving touch and contact at and immediately following birth, elsewhere referred to, hauls into question hospitals as appropriate birthing places. For sure, labor and delivery in high-risk pregnancies should occur in a place where the resources necessary to bring about safe delivery for mother and child are available. This means they should take place in a hospital. However, what about the 95% of normal deliveries? Should they not take place in a nurturing environment where the mother has known love and, hopefully, where the child has been conceived in love? For many years, there has been in place an efficient three-layered approach to the management of all pregnancies. Surely we can continue to plug into those fine systems that were created thirty years or more ago, so that unexpected difficulties can be handled at a moment's notice and the mother transferred to a place where she can be safely delivered. As birthers, women have much to ask themselves in terms of the power they have given away and which they need to reclaim over the birthing process. Indeed, one has to wonder about the long-term effects of depression and anxiety that result from women having had, as it were, the natural approach to childbirth taken away from them, a question not to be answered quickly, but one that surely deserves attention. In this regard, although there has been an understandable outcry over insurance companies limiting hospital stay for delivery to 24-hours, based of course on financial considerations and the historic trend to devalue the health of women and children by saving on their needs first, the move could have positive outcomes-*only, but only*, if women see and seize the opportunity to lobby for home delivery with qualified midwives. We will see, but meanwhile given the power of obstetrical status quo we should not hold our breath.

## *Woman as Nurturer*

Beginning with the basics, what about breast-feeding? Have women been seduced by advertising techniques and the blitz of the baby food companies? Abundant research has confirmed that not only does breast-feeding allow bonding to occur between the mother and child, but it provides the best food the child can have in the first few months of its life. Human milk not only has all of the minerals, proteins, carbohydrates, and fats, in proper proportions for a human child, it carries the immune factors that no bottle can ever provide. Alas, the baby food companies trampled these facts by promoting their modified cow's milk and other products to the tune of enormous profits. But the fact remains, no matter how you try to humanize cow's milk, cow's milk was made for baby cows, and no matter how you alter it to try and make it like human milk, it can *never* be human milk. Likewise, baby foods prepared and canned in factories have taken away the joy of preparing food as nurturance for children, better by far, prepared in the kitchen of the home than in a factory. The messages to women are not so subtle. As nurturers, they are considered inadequate. And then, throughout the childhood years, high-tech advertising instructs mothers on how to feed and clothe their children and school systems tell them what their children should learn without much reference to the nurturing of their souls and the balance that should exist between their minds, bodies, and souls. These, and other issues, impact on how women are denied the chance of being nurturers, not only to their children and families, but to themselves - a situation to which other factors also contribute.

In recent years the so-called Feminist Movement and the perceptions and misperceptions about it have added to this confusion. There is an eternal conflict between pursuing a sense of well-being through self-identity gained through accomplishment in the workplace versus a sense of well-being through the relationships we form. In general, women find identity in relationships. However, the so-called woman's revolution of the last several decades has invited, or should I say pushed women, to find identity outside of relationships within the family and the home. By working outside of the home, women have to seek self-identity within that environment which is predominately a male way of finding meaning. Many women who work outside of the home feel in the depth of their souls a kind of emptiness and some believe, as I do, that this is why many creative women, in particular, suffer from chronic depression. From earliest times, the feminine has added gentleness, wholeness, and earthly wisdom to the human experience. Frequently gentleness is partially, if not totally, absent from the work environment. When this happens, there is a silence within the soul. In order to succeed in the work environment, women are pushed to lose touch with their femininity. A man in his own world expects to receive from a woman emotional and practical support in his pursuit of identity through his work. When women are in the workplace, they also need, but from all accounts seldom receive, the same emotional and practical support from the men in their lives. Furthermore, when women are in this conflictual situation, the shadow side of striving for one's personal identity emerges. The shadow side is felt when one fails to attain the success one expected and/or the sense of achievement and wellbeing that is often projected to it. This, alas, is not an uncommon occurrence among women in the workplace. Shadow creates a sense of failure, and failure leads to guilt. Guilt creates fear and fear is the footprint of depression and anxiety. This, of course, impacts in a heavy and negative way on a woman's ability to find identity through relationships which is her natural way of doing so. So women are not only put into a bind when they work outside the home seeking identity, but given that their natural instinct is to find identity through relationships they have the double consequence of shame and guilt if they perceive themselves as not succeeding in either role. Women come into this world with a psyche imprinted with archetypal impressions. When there is conflict, women mourn for their lost femininity which they sense in their souls. This conflict, and its manifold fallout, is of very real concern in terms of women's sense of well-being. It gives rise to identity, emotional, and personality problems which contribute in great measure to the stress underlying all women's health issues. Woman as nurturer must think in terms of nurturing herself as well as her children and her spouse. This brings me back to the first point I made - that unless women identify whom they are as women, and unless they can be intimate with that and themselves, then true intimacy with another can never be fully achieved.

Women also need to be nurturers to other women. Are the stories of Cinderella and Red Shoes still alive and well today? I believe they are. In the many journals that I read, I have been very dismayed in recent years at the stories of young women in training to be physicians who are not only subjected to the hazing of male medical students, but have to run the gauntlet of what is perceived to be competition for these Prince Charmings on the part of other female health workers in more traditional professions. For example, we all love nurses, but there is a particular energy that goes between nurses and female medical students, young female physicians and indeed older ones as well. Endless articles have been written recently about it, the genesis of which I believe lies in the Cinderella story, every woman wanting the same Prince Charming, but I believe it may be also deeper than that, honing in on the trans-generational belief that men provide women with their identity. Frequently when women seek their identity and the use of their god given talents in spheres until recently open only to men, they are perceived by other women as stepping beyond the bounds of what women should do and be. But for the many the more status a man is perceived as having, the more he *appears* desirable to women who will then, as it were, assume some of his identity. Then again, how many times does one hear of women in high positions having difficulty finding a female secretary, not because there is anything the matter with the high achieving woman, but just on instinct and impulse when a woman hears that her boss is going to be a woman, she will frequently bow out of the picture even though she hasn't even met the woman who was going to be her boss. The heavier the reputation a woman has, the more creative she is, the more paranoia she creates in women who have not traveled her journey. A woman who embraces the ultimate in following her brilliance and her desire to find identity not only through her personal and professional achievements but in her relationships is most truly a great heroine, the feminine archetype of Joseph Campbell's concept of hero/heroine. It is one of the most difficult of human journeys in *every culture* today.

Many books have been written about how women are conditioned to think about other women - "Mothers and Daughters" and "The Cinderella Story," are two examples among many others. A profound question that hovers over the inability of women to accept and be nurturing toward other women is that, although they outnumber men, they are perceived and referred to as a minority. This belief sets up those who refuse to accept a minority role as target for defamation by those who do. Does the old adage, divide and conquer, apply to us women? I think the answer is obvious. Does this not have profound implications for women's identity? And does it not also cause suffering to those who refuse to surrender whom they are and their unique identity?

Certainly it does.

Pondering all this invites one to think about what it has done to the feminine psyche. Years ago, I had a very dear friend who was the director of social work at a large hospital; one day when we were talking in a semi-counseling session, she said, "I just feel that I am schizophrenic." She was, of course, not schizophrenic in the clinical sense of the word, but what she was referring to was the constant conflict and confusion about whom she was as a woman living in a man's world and trying at the same time to maintain and retain emotional relationships with herself, her family, and with the rest of the world. Does that cause stress? Of course, it does, and when stress is present, dysfunction of one kind or another ensues.

## *Woman as Crone*

The third part of the trinity of woman, is that of the Crone, the wise, older woman. The woman who endures and who responds to the feminine within her soul during the endurance test that is her life, does become the Crone. Although many women yield to the temptation to give their power away to men, particularly men of money and power, there are many women who instinctively know, and others who come to know by experience, that money, power, and authority are masks. These women realize at some point or other in their lives that true power lies within one's self and that each of us is a part of the expression of the Great Creator, the great, divine, creative Spirit. This divine spark lies at the core of our being and when we relinquish the pursuit of knowing, nurturing and loving that deepest part of ourselves which resides within our soul and is our eternal spirit we lose our comfort and our meaning. When women reclaim it, they are on the road to wisdom, to becoming the crone, the wise, older woman, the one who has the answers of peace and acceptance to life, its joys and its tragedies.

The tragedies of life result mostly from our sense of separation from the source of our being, which is love and creation. This separation can be self-inflicted as well as being the consequence of what life from the time of our conception does to us, or, as is more common, by both. In passing, I would like to make reference to what I think is a common misconception about creating our own reality. This is an often-talked-about topic these days and I think it has some danger in terms of laying guilt on those who seem unable to control the realities of their lives. The reality is that we often have little or no control over the things that occur in our lives. For example, we have little or no control over natural disasters or accidents nor of what happens to other people. However, we do in great measure have control and can exert control over our reactions to these events. It is when we realize that *we do have the inner wisdom* to monitor our reactions that we begin to be in touch with the wise older woman, the crone deep within ourselves. Those who have moved through these times of trial respond to the invitation of the infinite to grow beyond circumstance to the knowing of the great darkness, which to our limited human vision is infinity. Infinity itself lies beyond the illumination of suffering, but, the journey is never easy and in some instances well nigh impossible, as it is for too many women at the dawn of the 21st century

# VII

## *The Consciousness of Woman, Present Experience and Future Possibilities*

For most of the world's women, moving through their dispossession of self and self-identity to possession of self and self-identity remains an elusive dream. Evidence of their continued and frequent brutalization almost staggers the imagination. For example, just before the fourth U.N. World Conference on Women held in September 1995 in Bejing, China, Amnesty International proposed four urgent lines of action to secure equal justice and human rights for women. They were:

- Expose the worldwide scandal of escalating sexual torture and sustained abuse of women in both peace and war periods.

- Confront government indifference and complicity in encouraging the abuse of women around the world.

- Publicize the brutal violations against individual women and step up urgent actions on their behalf.

- Press government authorities to promote women's basic human rights and petition for the swift delivery of protection for women at risk.

The report went on to say that women have become, among other things, the invisible victims of the 1990s: the primary casualties of war; 80% of the world's refugees, and the target of human rights violations on a horrifying scale. Amnesty's 135-page report on the global condition of women's human rights, their graphic case studies and the damning country reports, have already begun to expose what is nothing less than a worldwide scandal.[1]

In wars and civil conflicts, women are often targeted for reprisal killings and singled out for rape and sexual assault which, increasingly, has become a weapon of war. The discriminatory treatment of women in many countries means they are more likely to suffer abuses that are not treated as crimes and that they will be far less likely to have these abuses exposed. These abuses are legion: women are raped in custody, are forced to take virginity tests by police, they are flogged for violating dress codes, and even risk being stoned to death for "sexual offenses." The abuse of women remains not only largely hidden but also largely ignored by world governments. Many governments, who only recently adopted the "U.N. Declaration on the Elimination of all Forms of Violence Against Women," continue to be responsible for appalling and increasing levels of violence against them. Women who have experienced sexual torture and other abuse pay the price with lifelong psychological damage, serious physical injury, pregnancy, disease, and death. In her memoir, *Do They Hear You When You Cry*, Fauzia Kassindja, a native of Togo in West Africa, gives a human face to the torture of the blood-soaked ritual of Kakia, otherwise known as female genital mutilation, which is widely practiced throughout the world. She recounts that four women spread your legs wide apart, hold you down, and scrape away all your woman parts. After forty days, you are "reborn" for your husband and delivered to his house. Thankfully, women are finding a voice to protest and bring to an end this barbaric torture. In other countries where low wages, long hours, and sexual harassment are typical of their working conditions, some women have found the strength to organize and begin changing their situation, despite threats of firing, blackmail, and even death. These abuses have a tremendous fallout not only in the personal suffering of women, but on their children, families, and ultimately on society.

Albeit with an emphasis on Western women, this has been admirably addressed by Dr. Christine Northrup in her best-selling book *Women's Bodies; Women's Wisdom*. Citing "Toxic People" from past or present, "Toxic Thoughts,

---

[1]Taken from a memorandum to all Amnesty Members from William E. Schultz, Executive Director [June 22, 1995]

Attitudes and Ideas" about "a woman's place" as central to most physical illness, she documents incontrovertible evidence of how women are ignored, neglected, or at best patronized by the medical establishment.[2] While they account for half of all visits to physician's offices, women receive 83 % of all prescriptions for anti-depressant drugs - surely a brush-off for real problems of *soul* that results in three-quarters of all patients in mental hospitals being women. Is this to be wondered at when half of all women and children in the U.S.A. are victims of domestic violence, and that the number of women who die as a result of spousal and family violence in any five-year period in the U.S.A. equals or is in excess of all American fatalities in the Vietnam War? The latter have a monument to their memory in Washington, D.C., but there are no monuments to these women, only the transgenerational continuance of what was done to them as memories in the individual consciousness of their children and the collective consciousness of society, which, of course, serves to perpetuate the problems.

There is much evidence to support this. Children of battered women have significantly more developmental, learning, and behavioral problems than do children who have not experienced this trauma. I have no doubt that if this is put into the context of memory and consciousness, these sequelae are due to changes in the energy patterns of memory that ultimately impact negatively on the genes that influence and/or control these functions. The pivotal role of the mother's emotional health and stability in the health and welfare of her children has been abundantly documented. Indeed, the authors of a study carried out in New Zealand and reported in *Pediatrics* in 1984 concluded that the major contributing factor to problems in child rearing was maternal depression brought on by negative family-life events.[3] Other research has shown time and again that even the smallest of infants are so highly attuned to the moods of their parents, especially those of their mother, that when mother-child interactions are interfered with by the mother's depression, their infants respond by showing sadness, social withdrawal, and helplessness, the latter being an early sign of learning impairment. Just how

[2] Christine Northrup, *Women's Bodies, Women's Wisdom*. (New York: Bantam Books, 1994).
[3] D.M. Ferguson et al., *Relationship of Family Life Events, Maternal Depression and Child Rearing Problems*, in Pediatrics 73, 6, June 1984.

devastating this is to the quality of collective consciousness is reflected in the fact that by global estimates 1 in 3 women are victims of physical beatings.

*As a consequence in 2000 the United Nations called for domestic violence to be declared a global health problem, and for appropriate action to be taken.*

To the best of my knowledge at the time of this writing, this call to action still awaits implementation.

Yet, despite the abundance of knowledge we have about the importance of maternal health of body, mind, and soul, not only for themselves but also for their children, so far the emphasis has been on physical health while the beat goes on with the denouement of emotional and spiritual well-being. A study conducted by Lois Weiss, Ph.D. of the University at Buffalo Graduate School of Education, and Michelle Fine of CUNY Graduate School revealed what the authors described as a horrific picture of women's lives saturated with serious domestic violence.[4]

Ninety-two percent (92%) of white female respondents said that serious domestic violence was directed against them, their mothers, and/or sisters either in their birth households or in later relationships. Serious domestic violence was defined as battering intended to cause serious physical injury. By comparison, 62 % of black female respondents reported similar levels of violence in their lives. Furthermore, while black women were not secretive either in personal interviews or group sessions, white women spoke openly only in private sessions. The authors observed that one way white women maintain their racial difference is to cultivate the popular cultural image of the perfectly functioning white nuclear family, a lie and maybe a survival mechanism as highlighted by the following advice in the Toronto Globe and Mail of July 17, 1996.

In an article titled "When the First Man Turns You Away," it was poignantly stated that,

*"If the one man who is supposed to provide you (the female) with unconditional love withholds affection it becomes a deeply ingrained habit to wonder what is intrinsically wrong with you; to wonder if others can see it as*

---

[4] Lois Weiss and Michelle Fine, The Unknown City: The Lives of Poor and Working Class Young Adults. (Beacon Press: New York, 1998).

*well and then fight, inexhaustibly, to either prove them wrong
or prove them right - but at least prove you're worth attention.
Thus, abusive relationships become the norm because you
know what to expect from them - the familiarity assures you
that you belong in them. And echoing what I have heard so
often from my clients," she added, "Mothers loved us deeply
but not enough to see the damage being done and not
enough to choose us over him. Brothers perceive this also
and practice the callousness they've been taught by their
male role models - expecting to be loved, nurtured and oh,
yes, even adored - regardless their behavior because, well,
isn't this the way their mothers (loved) endured their fathers.*

In this regard, I have often been made keenly aware
of how men compartmentalize their relationships with
women: extending respect and devotion to their mothers
versus disrespect and often abuse to all others. It is a
theme brilliantly and often humorously addressed by Dr.
Rafael Lopez-Corvo in his book *God Is a Woman*, in which
he explores the power that women exert over men.[5] He
argues that the violence toward women is based on man's
eternal longing for his mother and envy of woman's ability
to bear children, sentiments I myself have frequently heard
expressed by men. He suggests that women should search
for their own identity, a pursuit that I heartily endorse, and
he suggests they should find a place where God could be a
woman. I myself believe that when the collective
consciousness reaches a critical point as a result of women
discovering, encountering and living their identity, then
reverence for the feminine will be reestablished and
restored. Perhaps, then, this will become as he hopes the
place and the point in time where God will be perceived as a
woman, but meanwhile, it is quite evident that we have far
to travel to that expectantly golden world. Better still one
wherein the Godhead is perceived as;

**ONE INDIVISIBLE FEMININE AND MASCULINE ENERGY.**

Statistics in the U.S. reveal that battering accounts
for 1 out of 5 women seeking medical care, as well as the
reason for up to thirty five percent (35%) of their visits to
hospital emergency rooms. Yet, if one looks only for
physical trauma in these situations, the vast majority of

---

[5] Rafael Lopez-Corvo, *God Is a Woman.* (Northvale, NJ: Jason Aronson,
1997).

battered women will be overlooked. Violence in the home often manifests as anxiety, depression, chemical dependency, chronic headaches, sleeping and eating disorders, a wide variety of somatic complaints, as well as suicide attempts. The dynamic in battering and violence is power and control over the victim which is often reinforced by the victim's fear of reprisals should they report it to the authorities. It is common knowledge that at the scene of domestic assaults, victims often beg police not to arrest their batterer, and in courts women frequently demand that charges against their tormentors be dropped. The tragedy is that most women in these situations realize that no matter what they do, they are in danger of their lives. Most abusers justify their disgusting behavior by blaming it on some perceived flaw in their victims; in so doing, they hold their victim responsible for the violence. "Look what you made me do" is the statement an abuser frequently makes after a violent episode in which he has physically, verbally, and emotionally abused a woman or a child.

Fifty percent (50%) of all women murdered in the U.S. are killed by a current or former partner, Yet, if we look for a concerted and focused effort to halt this physical, emotional, spiritual, and transgenerational carnage, there is none. Rather, there are a few programs scattered here and there that jab at one or another aspect of the overall problem. A few of these are educational in the sense that they seek to change attitudes prevalent in society that identifies women as sub-human or at best not in any way equal to men. By de-personalizing women, such beliefs make it easier to be abusive of them; after all, hitting a peer or one's equal is so rare it makes news! Such depersonalization is fostered and promoted by the lucrative pornography industries all over the world that portray mutilation and torture of women and children as a male sport. Sexual fantasies and stories of women being kidnapped, sodomized, mutilated, and left to die by men who show no remorse are creeping on to the Internet. That sexual fantasy turns into sexual abuse is still being debated, though one wonders why. As Catherine MacKinnon, a law professor and a leader in advocacy for women's rights and author of *Only Words*, states: "Writing and reading pornography are in themselves acts of violence." Further evidence of the dispensability of women and children is reflected in a recent UNICEF bulletin which stated that in the so-called Third World in 1997, an estimated six million or more children were starving and because of discrimination against women and their low status, leading to poor nutrition, millions more were born prematurely with all of its attendant risks and many others were born with crippling conditions.

Within all of this, it is easy to discern the legacy of Eve and her counterparts in other cultures. Blame continues to be placed on women for the problems of men, and because of her inferiority, woman is subject to his power, control, and usage. At this point, it is well to keep in mind what has already been addressed, that the tale of Creation and the expulsion from the Garden of Eden are in scriptural texts written by men and only about four thousand years or less ago, which in terms of human evolution is a mere blink in the march of time. The prodigious accomplishments and research of the brilliant scholar, archeologist, and linguist Dr. Marija Gimbutas, who recently died, leave no doubt that prior to Old Testament times, women were revered as the soul of creation. Indeed, woman was the goddess on whom all life depended and from whom all life flowed.[6]

As to why such a drastic change in the relationship of male and female occurred the causes are probably many. In addition to the possibilities previously mentioned, it is not beyond feasibility that within the context of the evolution of human consciousness, the emergence and dominance of ego could well have caused male rebellion against the power of the female. Her power was vested in her fecundity and her beauty, and it was this that men sought to control. That this continues is evident from the dominance and control sought by men who preside over the political, cultural, and religious dimensions of most societies over the wonders, beauty, and fecundity of women's bodies. The international trade of women for sex amounting to countless billions of dollars for their pimps is matched only by the powerless-ness and despair women too often experience in regard to control over their reproductive capacities. Over time, it is conceivable that the biology of

---

[6] See Marija Gimbutas, *The Bronze Age Cultures of Central and Eastern Europe.* (Mouton: The Hague, 1965); *The Language of the Goddess.* (San Francisco: Harper, 1991) and *Civilization of the Goddess.* (San Francisco: Harper, 1991).

the male and his greater physical strength married to his ego succeeded in making him dominant. Once able to intimidate the female verbally and physically, it was a short step to casting his dominance in stone and this was cleverly accomplished by invoking the imprimatur of the Goddess herself, clothed now in a male image by male dominated beliefs and religions who removed her from the Godhead, making it all male. Armed with this permission, male hegemony straddled and strangled the feminine by assuming control over the source of her power, which is creation, and so it has been since the days wherein the Old Testament was written. We live in an era where this is all too visible. Men not only make laws about the OUTCOME of sexual encounters between themselves and women, but laws that punish the women but NOT the men if they disobey their dictates.

It is evident that once blame on women and their subservience to men was codified in religious texts, which incidentally are curiously silent about male responsibility for the consequences of sexual activity, the stage was set for their exploitation. Proclaiming God, who was now male, as the source of their authority, men passed laws and organized society to ensure their dominance. Women were denied rights to property and self-realization and were considered chattels to be used, abused, and controlled by men who exercised total power over them. At the core of this tragedy was the loss of ownership of their own bodies and souls, a fact that in the 19th century made the great lady Florence Nightingale observe, "Today is my 30th birthday and I am glad that those years wherein a woman owns nothing, not even her own soul, are now behind me." She was, of course, mis-taken; for, in spite of her great accomplishments, not only in nursing, but in concern for social issues, she continued to 'face and battle put-downs from men, much less gifted than she was until the end of her life.

While the scriptural story of Adam and Eve is the prototype of what has been the "norm" over the past several millennia in the Judeo Christian tradition, and which still continues, is it to be wondered that in societies regarded as being religious in the sense of CHURCH AND RITUAL controlling the masses, the abuse of women and children is endemic? An article in the February 22, 1998 issue of the

*Manchester Guardian Weekly,* U.K. addressed what is happening in Poland. The headline stated: "Women in Poland Lose Habit of Submission." To address the epidemic of domestic violence, the Center for Human Rights was established in Warsaw just two years ago by Ursula Nowakowska. Her aim was to drive into the public domain an issue, which from time immemorial was considered a private, family matter. A hotline established for victims is being hassled by men who call for an end to this meddling in "their" private affairs. Most significantly, and recently, a government office for women and children has been replaced by an office for *family affairs* and is headed by an archconservative male. And, yet, just a few years ago, a Polish Pope revealed his conversion to the plight of women by calling on men to be more involved with their families and the loving raising of their children. Evidently, that message has yet to reach his homeland! In revealing his conversion, the Pope said, "... When one looks at the great process of women's liberation, the journey has been a difficult and complicated one ... substantially a positive one, *even if it is still unfinished.*"[7] Those of us who remember and felt the pain of how, on his first visit to the United States, Pope John Paul II crudely and rudely dismissed the women who reverently asked for a voice in the church of which they are the majority, can only point to his conversion as what is possible when one becomes enlightened.

The systematic erosion of the feminine and abuse of her identity is deeply embedded in the memory and soul of every woman. Therefore, when they say, "I don't know who I am," they are proclaiming what the loss of feminine identity has wrought. Additionally, on an individual level this injury to collective consciousness interplays with personal experience to create the *power-less-ness* at the center of so much anguish and morbidity experienced by women.

HOWEVER, THIS IS NOT ALL.

The male who abuses the female does violence to his own soul and, in so doing, further distances himself from his original identity of at-one-ment with his Creator. Furthermore, by witnessing violence in the place where

---

[7] Pope John Paul 11, Easter Address to Priests, 1997.
Note: Please see Appendix item 4 for information on grassroots programs developed to enfranchise and empower women.

there should be love and respect, horrendous injuries are inflicted on the souls of children, whose memories persist forever. These memories and the anxiety, depression, and despair that violence generates become the precursors of its transmission from generation to generation. These are the scars on the souls of humankind - men, women and children, *everywhere*. Their healing requires far more than the bandages we presently apply to them. In fact, what is needed is nothing less than a radical transformation of our attitudes and a rekindling of respect for "She," without whom there would be no men. In so doing, humankind must seek to recreate the holy and wholesome alliance of male and female and, thus, send the light of this one-ness as a message of hope and love to humankind. First, however, we must be about educating all children, male and female, about the beauty and the spirit of the feminine. Even if we could start now, it will take two to three generations before the critical level of changed memories and their energies become perceptible. This endeavor can only be enhanced and enriched if we earnestly seek understanding of what children themselves have been subjected to in the pursuit of wealth, power, and status for men, a territory we will now explore.

# VIII

## *Children Past and Present*
## *Their Use, Abuse, and Expendability*

The world of children is filled with contradictions. There are, and always have been, un-countable numbers of un-wanted children. Indeed willful killing of infants and children, usually girls, has been responsible for more child deaths than any other single cause in history, other than possibly the bubonic plague.[1,2] At the present time Millions who have been abandoned, eke out an existence on the streets of some of the major cities of the world, where they roam in bands seeking to steal for subsistence, thus terrorizing the citizenry and, in turn, being terrorized and even gunned down by law enforcement agencies who perceive them as human garbage.

Yet obversely, people expend themselves and their energies in fundraising activities to find cures for childhood diseases and not always because they are parents of an afflicted child. Others volunteer love and time to make summer camps and other activities available to poor children, as well as those with chronic and life-threatening diseases. When a child is in danger, no effort is spared for its rescue. When a child dies, whether close or far, relative, friend or stranger, many of us grieve. Similarly, with great fanfare, governments underwrite programs, amounting to billions of dollars, to ensure that all children are immunized against physical disease when, in fact, immunization levels are the highest on record and statistics tell us that physical diseases are no longer the killers of children.

If this be so, then what are the current killing fields of children?

---

[1] Theodore Solomon, *History and Demography of Child Abuse*, Pediatrics, April 1973

[2] Samuel X. Radbill, *A History of Child Abuse and Infanticide and Violence in the Family*, (New York: Mead and Company, 1973).

One doesn't have to ponder long over available statistics to realize that child abuse and neglect are presently a worldwide epidemic. Abuse, whether it be verbal, emotional, physical, sexual, spiritual, or all of these, and the concomitant lack of respect and love in tandem with neglect and abandonment, are now the killers of children, and the slayers of the adults they become. Redressing these evils begs our urgent attention because these killers of the hearts, minds, and souls of children and the sense of power-less-ness and helplessness they engender, journey with them into adolescence and adulthood. There they manifest in all manner of psychiatric (i.e. soul) disorders and ultimately light the fire of rage that spews itself on the world as terror and violence. In searching for the origins of child abuse, sadly but not surprisingly, one finds them in the belief systems of most cultures and religions. Historically these have perceived children, on the one hand as vessels in need of correction and discipline (meaning abuse) and on the other, as chattels to be used as cheap or slave labor, both commercially and domestically. By turning blind eyes, either willfully or because of ignorance to what was taking place, societies in general, have for centuries granted permission for the de-valuation of children as unique human and spiritual beings, reinforcing the political, cultural, and religious climates that permitted it and within which it still continues.

Opening the historical door wider on the abuse of children reveals that the whipping of children and youth, has since the days of the early Greeks, been regarded as the prerogative of parents and teachers. The intent was to whip them into submission; but what it actually accomplished was the perpetuation of this violence through the energy of the *memories* it created in its victims who, not uncommonly, developed sadomasochistic tendencies which were deposited on the bodies and souls of future generations. The extent of sexual abuse of children is reflected in the reports of Greek and Roman doctors who rarely found intact hymens in female children. The rape of little girls was so common that scenes built around such incidents were a mainstay of ancient comedies and were considered to be the "funny" highlights of these stage plays. Likewise, boys were regularly handed over by their parents to neighboring men to be used for adult sexual pleasure. Indeed, Plutarch wrote a long essay on the best kind of person to choose for such activities at a time when child brothels, rent-a-boy services and sex slavery flourished. In ancient times, it was common practice for parents to hand over their children at birth to caretakers, a precursor of the nursemaid and nanny practices of later generations. However, in ancient times, it was common practice for these caretakers to abuse the children sexually and no doubt, also physically. In Colonial America, adolescents could legally be hanged for cursing or smiting their natural parents in contexts where these youths were probably rebelling against being used and abused. From their inception, schools have often been the location of violence toward youth, many employing a man in charge of the whip to punish schoolboys upon the slightest pretext.[3] This sadomasochism was undoubtedly the acting out of memories of abuse in the whipper's own childhood, a manifestation of the power of transgenerational memory and its residence in the collective consciousness. The history of children is filled with reports of nightmares, hallucinations, and terrors, as well as convulsing fits, dancing manias, loss of hearing and speech, and confessions of intercourse with devils. The attitude of parents and caretakers toward these events was reflective of their own childhood experiences - for rather than giving comfort, they believed the best way for the children to overcome their fears and problems was to confront them head-on. They would take children to cemeteries and to gibbets from which hung the rotting corpses of those recently publicly hanged - most often for stealing to survive - and to prisons where prisoners were whipped and tortured.[4] In hindsight, many of the afflictions these children were enduring were due to diseases such as Saint Vitus' dance and other neurological disorders. It is a fact that historically and throughout the world parents have tended to wield absolute power over the lives of their children, even unto death if they were unwanted. The socio-cultural roots of this power sprang from many sources but most particularly from beliefs inculcated by religion, as well

---

[3] Theodore Solomon, *History and Demography of Child Abuse*, Pediatrics, April 1973;
[4] Samuel X. Radbill, *A History of Child Abuse and Infanticide and Violence in the Family*, (New York: Mead and Company, 1973).

as concern for population control, and maintenance of a physically healthy, i.e, able to work, population.[5]

*The extent of parental power has led some to conclude that the history of humanity is founded on the abuse of this power as visited as abuse on children.*

Reader, take a moment and a deep breath to digest what this means.

The messages in this book and others that I have written points to my belief that this is correct. The rationale for such a stunning statement includes the fact that just as family therapists today find that child abuse often functions to hold families together as a way of solving their emotional problems, so too, the routine assault of children has been society's most effective way of maintaining its collective homeostasis.

***Just imagine homeostasis - meaning, same state - achieved through violence against children. This in itself stuns the mind and sensitivities if we have eyes and ears to see and hear what its real meaning is! But, alas its fallout has stunned and stunted the soul of humankind.***

Concern for this carnage began in Europe about three and a half centuries ago and gained momentum in the 19th century through the writings of Charles Dickens and others which eventually led to social reforms.   These reforms rarely if ever, penetrated the fortress of the home. . Undoubtedly, the prevailing dominance placed on the rights of parents and the lower public visibility of what went on behind closed doors, contributed to the uninhibited and unrestricted practice of violence in the home, to the point where it was accepted as standard behavior. So great were parental rights that in 1874, in Boston, Massachusetts, when the celebrated case of Mary Ellen took place, she was removed from the appalling abuse and neglect to which she was subjected, in her home, by virtue of legislation designed to protect animals, there being no such legislation at that time to protect children. Strange and appalling as it may seem, it was legislated concern for animal welfare, combined with outrage at the unprecedented publicized

---

[5]David Bakin, Slaughter of the Innocents: A Study of the Battered Child, (Boston: Beacon Press, 1972).

anguish of one child, that eventually led to the establishment of child protection programs, whose mission today is overwhelmed by the sheer numbers of children needing their services.

Yet in spite of historical realities about the abuse of children, somehow a popular image has emerged that threads its way into the popular belief that children safely belong to and in the HOME and FAMILY. Alas this vision is dimmed by current realities and statistics that make of it a mirage.

- In the USA in 1998, 615,336 school age children were reported as HOME-LESS and approximately 18% were NOT enrolled in school during their home-less-ness. In addition, 205,749 pre-school children were reported as homeless.[6]

- In 2000, 556,000 children were in foster care.

- In 2000, 2,796,000, i.e. nearly 3 million children, were referred to agencies for possible neglect and abuse.

- In 2000, approximately 4 million children younger than age 6 were living below the poverty level.

- In 2001, 8.5 million children were without medical insurance.

- Each year it is estimated that between 2 and 3 million children witness some form of domestic violence.[7]

Worldwide, children are becoming the unwanted legacies of ethnic and religious wars due to rape and murder, leaving them without shelter or food.

The staggering number of unwanted children now on the streets and by-ways of the world means that the future of these millions of children are being jeopardized and destroyed by forces over which they have no control.

---

[6] National Center for Homeless Education, Washington, D.C.
[7] Child Welfare League of America

The short-sightedness of a society that fails to take into account its own well-being by not addressing the soul distress of children was referred to by Van Doom Ooms in a recent article which analyzed current fiscal policy in the United States. He said that by not adequately addressing the increase in child poverty, the productivity of the future labor force is threatened. This is an interesting comment because for all the abuse and usage children endured in the past, they were nevertheless perceived as immediately essential to the money economy and the building of Empire. Nowadays, their input is more remote given laws designed to prohibit their employment until adolescence and the expectation they will be in school until aged 17 or 18, alas, an unfulfilled expectation, especially for homeless children. Remote though their future employment may appear to a society bent on immediate profits, children are the future workforce for a workplace that will demand skills and knowledge far beyond what these dis-enfranchised children will be able to offer. Then, there are the throwaway kids, those who have been told to leave home or have been thrown out by their parents and the more than one million who run away each year often to escape abuse. In her book *Please Help Me God*, Sister Mary Rose McGready, former President of Covenant House in the U.S.A., America's largest shelter for homeless and runaway kids, tells the heartbreaking stories of some of these children. Entangled in a web of abuse and sex, these innocents, some as young as 10 years of age, struggle to find hope in the dark and loveless world of their knowing. But, as testimony to the love that does exist in our world, hundreds of people of all ages have dedicated themselves to helping these children and have formed Covenant House Faith Community in order to do so. Many of these volunteers live in community for 13 months and work one-on-one with the children. One has to wish that even some of the half-million youth who are incarcerated in secure facilities for MAJOR crimes such as murder had somehow found their way to one of the several locations of Covenant House and other similar resources. The inability of many children and youth to find meaning in their lives is at the root of the so-called "new" morbidities of youth such as school failure; 25% of high school-students drop out of school every year; Violence; and the addictions of sex, drugs, and alcohol. In fact all of these are their cry for direction and their yearning to find the meaning that is all too absent from their lives.

There has been and continues to be much discussion as to the causes of these human agonies and tragedies and the failure of current approaches to remediation. But if we put these issues into the context of the power of *trans-generational memory*, both personal and collective, we begin to unfold the answers we seek and thereby are enabled to stand on the threshold of,

### WHY WE ARE THE WAY WE ARE.

It is almost a century since Carl Jung and others told us that all experience becomes a component of collective consciousness and though we have been slow learners in generally applying this knowledge **in no other sphere of human existence** is this more true, and more deeply engraved, than that of how children have in the past been regarded and treated. Indeed these *trans-generational memories* are the building blocks upon which every generation has based its belief systems, adding and subtracting to them as society, cultures, and religious beliefs have changed. The importance of this can not be overstated, because abundant evidence indicates that adult attitudes and behavior, particularly the texture of our interactions and responses to others and to life situations is woven from the memories of our early experience. As previously described, these begin at conception and proceed through pregnancy, birth, infancy, and early childhood. The energies that this blend of memories generate in the trinity of mind, body, and soul both individually and collectively become the motor that drives thoughts, feelings, and behavior. Thus if we change the quality of energy within the collective consciousness which dictates the belief systems of society, this will, by absorption, as it were, find a lodging in the consciousness of individuals.

Similarly, by changing the quality of energies within individuals these alterations will flow into the collective consciousness; in other words changing one leaves imprints on the other. The potential for moderating intolerance, hatred, and other negative and destructive energies is obvious.

The great Indian sage Krishnamurti said it well:

*"When one becomes aware of ones conditioning, then it is possible to understand the whole of ones consciousness."*

To which I would add - and that of others and nations as well.

But how do we accomplish this?

# IX

## *Immunizing the Soul*
## *Balancing Inner and Outer Ecology*

If we accept the fact that the mind and soul have immune systems much like those of the physical body, then we must find ways to immunize them against what injures or deadens them; much like what takes place when we immunize people, particularly children against infectious diseases.[1]  These biological vaccines are derived from the micro-organisms that cause infections after their aggressive and often lethal properties have been attenuated by the use of heat and other means.  These attenuating processes change the *memories* of their engagement with their hosts by physically changing the molecular and other locks and keys that allow them to latch on to the cells of their hosts. These altered *memories* change their energies from aggressive frequencies that cause infection to those that are more benign, which latter allow the immune system of their hosts to manufacture defenses against them.  In contemporary lingo these phenomena could be described as changes in the Inner Ecology of both the attacker and attackee.

In this regard it is worth noting that newer vaccines are being developed without particles of cellular matter, which in fact and reality makes of these vaccines vehicles of the *Energies* of the micro-organisms rather than vehicles of their cellular matter.  For these a-cellular vaccines to be effective, and experience proves that they are, it must be that the ENERGIES of the MEMORIES of these organisms are able to engage the ENERGIES in the immune systems of their hosts thereby creating defense mechanisms to repel future invasions.

The spectacular success of immunization in the control, and in some cases, eradication of infectious

---

[1] See website of author, www.drursulaanderson.com, originator of the concept of immune systems for mind and soul.

diseases which until recently were the major killers of humankind cannot be denied. The statistics speak for themselves. For example, Figure I [Appendix] shows the dramatic effect of immunization on infectious rates for Poliomyelitis and Figure II [Appendix] shows what immunization did to control infection rates for diptheria.

Since we know that dysfunctional human behavior derives from the energies of injurious memories that drive thoughts, feelings, and behavior, surely it should be possible to transpose what happens in the establishment of physical immunity to that of mind and soul because the dynamic is essentially the same. In other words, we need to enable the Inner Ecology of the Soul to be functional.

Let me put this possibility into an analogous context. If we identify belief systems that are injurious to individuals or groups as the equivalent of the micro-organisms that cause physical disease, and if we can find ways to attenuate (i.e. moderate) these beliefs so as to minimize their impact, then it does become more than theoretical and even possible to identify ways and means to immunize the immune systems of mind and soul against their negative impacts, both individually and collectively.

Such possibilities and the changes in beliefs and attitudes that are necessary might at first appear to be a distant dream, but looking back just a century ago, the possibility of conquering infectious diseases, and the protection against them that we presently enjoy due to widespread immunization, was at that time thought to be a distant if not impossible dream. But the changes necessary to bring it about DID in fact take place.

Change in general is usually met with resistance and most particularly in the spheres of cultural and religious beliefs. In some ways this is beneficial providing as it does, time for reflection on the possible outcomes of change vis a vis the status quo which often has the appeal of continuity and the sense of security this conveys. But nature informs us throughout the seasons as does human development that change is necessary for growth, meaning that the inherent memories and energies of each interplay to form on the one hand landscapes and on the other individuals whose outer and inner identities change in response to the instinctive drive to grow and mature. In the normal course of events these changes move from one stage to the next in an orderly fashion. If at any point there is a delay or an assault on this dynamic, it will have a domino and delaying effect on subsequent stages ranging from mild to severe to lethal. This rule pervades every aspect of human development; physically, psychologically, emotionally, and spiritually, and relates not only to the individual but to humankind in general. Applying the concept of progressive change to the development of collective consciousness within the rubric of the stages of its evolutionary unfolding to an omega point of one-ness, and a felt connection to the source of love and creation which expresses itself in tolerance, respect, and compassion it would not be inappropriate to perceive it as being currently stalled, because the reality is that divisive cultural and religious beliefs are poisoning it with disrespect, hatred, violence, and terror. It is these negative and destructive cultural and religious beliefs that are the entities that need to be immunized by means that will attenuate their virulence.

But WHY should this horror, so foreign to the core tenets and aspirations of all religions and cultures be taking place. Like all behavior, it has to do with the power of *memory* and the *consciousness* that drives it.

From the beginning and no doubt until the end of time, every human being has searched and will continue to search for their personal connection to the divine. Seers and saints of all religions have for millennia given us prescriptions as to how to live our lives so that this oneness with the sources of creation can be attained and felt within our souls, to the point of wordlessly communicating the love and respect for all that it reflects. But along the way their messages and those of traditions as well as what is called revelation, have been interpreted and codified into belief systems that we call religions. These have evolved into institutions of power and control of the many by the few who claim to be custodians of the commands to love and be tolerant but who in fact have become in many instances unfeeling enforcers of beliefs that deny this love and tolerance to many.

A common belief of the hierarchies and ministers of religions and the several denominations and pathways within each, is that they alone harbor THE TRUTH and therefore all ideas, practices, and behavior that derive from their interpretation of it are considered non-negotiable. Furthermore, such beliefs and attitudes confer permission for them to perceive all other religions to be in error. Thus in the past and yes, even now, when they have engaged in discourse it frequently has not been with loving respect for each other, but in man made arguments designed to assure the maintenance of their respective positions of supremacy.

At the root of this play acting is fear of losing power, control, and the obedience of their adherents which of course embeds *separation from other* in their minds and souls and re-inforces the continuance of thinking and behaving fearfully. This emphasis on power, status, and authority, and the material gain that flows from them has dimmed the spirituality and yearning for oneness with GOD and OTHERS that lives deep in the soul of every human being. This is because programmed into their memory is the belief that God can only be reached through their religious leaders and clerics. Surely the time is NOW for those scientists, and others who have the knowledge of the emotional and spiritual pathology this stance is wreaking on humanity, to seek admission to their discourses in order to appraise them of it, and to question the origins of the beliefs they claim as their authority.

Of the many inequities and injustices male dominated religions and cultures have manufactured and perpetuated, ONE above all cries "SHAME ON YOU."

*It is the abuse of women and children, the idea that they are inferior beings and their relegation to subservient bondage to the whims, ambitions, and desires of men.*

The tenets on which such infamy was founded and allowed to persist are now being seriously questioned and re-examined, but their memories quite clearly remain in the collective consciousness and manifest themselves in patently open, as well as subtle ways. Witness the not so funny jokes intended as put-downs about the effects of a woman's hormonal cycle, without which in their arrogance and ignorance men forget they would never be born; the burden of proof placed on female victims of rape and the unbelieving attitudes of a "justice" system dominated by men who more often than not place blame for the rape on the victim herself, thus victimizing her twice; the cavalier attitude of men towards women they have impregnated when having "sex fun" and the shirking of their responsibility to her and the unborn child. The recent exposure about what happened to some of these unfortunate girls in Catholic Ireland during the 20th century and prior to it has shocked the world. Sent to institutions run by religious orders of nuns which were little more than prisons, they were in every way used and abused. Told that their sin had earned them eternal damnation and forced into unpaid labor 12 to 16 hours a day, these poor unfortunate children of God were damned, not by their so-called sin of pregnancy, which may have resulted from rape, but by those clothed in religious garb who treated them as garbage. But what about the males, young and old, who impregnated them? As far as we know, none were sent to correctional institutions for their abusive crimes against young women, nor were they used as forced and unpaid labor to expiate their sin, and certainly few or none as far as we know, came to claim the children they begat or care for the girls whose lives they ruined. And of course, let us here not forget the roles assigned to women in most religions. Until very recently excluded from performing sacred rituals or being ordained to do so, they were and still are expected to clean places of worship and the vessels, vestments, and linens used therein. Most of all, they were/are expected to be obedient to male directives.

This antipathy towards women and inability or refusal to respect their sacred identity and creative gifts is a deep sickness in the souls of men. Its fallout on the souls of women and the images they have of themselves plus the low self worth, depression, and anxiety that it causes profoundly influences the quality of their lives and the energies and attitudes they bring to motherhood and their responses and reactions to their children. For example, recent Studies[2] reveal that mothers in general, are more pessimistic in interactions with their daughters and more optimistic with their sons. As a consequence, by the time of mid adolescence the risk for depression in girls is double that for boys. Mothers quite obviously are responding to the cultural difference in the personal worth of male and

---

[2] Kimberly Driscoll. In Pediatric News August 2003. Paper presented to the Society for Research in Child Development. July 2003.

female and by so doing are passing these values on to future generations allowing boys and men to continue to devalue and use girls and women. In this case the power and impact of the Outer Ecology of attitudes, born of beliefs, on the Inner Ecology of women and its transmission to her children is clear to see.

When the consequences cause problems in healthy emotional and behavioral functioning, they have in the past and continue to be attributed to psychological and/or mental disturbances, which in a broad sense they are.

But at the dawn of the 21st century it is no secret that the litany of theories about human psychology which have ebbed and flowed along with the therapies believed to effectively deal with, if not heal, its pathology have for the most part, failed. James Hillman, a Jungian analyst, offers a disturbing commentary on this dilemma in his wonderfully titled book *"We've had a Hundred Years of Psychotherapy and the World is Still Getting Worse."* Recently alarm over the failure of mental health resources to meet the demands, let alone the needs, of children in their teens and younger has been expressed in both the United Kingdom and the United States. In the U.K. concern has also been voiced about inadequate resources for women.[3,4] At the root of these failures is the general inattention given to the interplay of soul with mind in the genesis of psycho-pathology, whereby the feeling part of us, *the soul*, becomes devitalized and its spiritual and resilient energies are weakened. Statistics tell us that the occurrence of what is referred to as mental illness but which in fact reflects *soul* disharmony is on the increase.

However I believe that the present mayhem and the inadequacies of treatment and therapy could eventually be the blessing that will invite SOUL into our consciousness as a dynamic force. This is so necessary because it is the functions of SOUL expressed as feelings and the functions of MIND expressed as thoughts and beliefs that are at the center of society's DYS-FUNCTION.

---

[3] Suzanne Boulter. *The Crisis in Pediatric Psychiatry* in PEDIATRIC NEWS. May 2002.
[4] *Mental Health Trusts Drowning in Debt.* THE INDEPENDENT ON SUNDAY June 15, 2002.

The concepts and values that have caused disturbances of Inner Ecology are firmly rooted in religious texts, ancient and modern, from whence they have flowed into the cultural beliefs and attitudes that permit and encourage their practices. Light has been shed on how this came about by the recent discovery of ancient texts which have lain fallow for millennia. Written by early followers of Jesus Christ, known as the GNOSTICS, these texts give different accounts of the founding of the early church than those found in the synoptic gospels upon which beliefs were dogmatized and organizations founded which have passed through countless generations to the present time.[5,6] A prominent difference relates to the crucial role that Mary Magdalen played in the life of Jesus and to correction of the image of a "fallen woman" conferred on her by prominent males of the early church. Suppression of these Gnostic gospels by the male leaders of the early church and probably Peter, the first pope, from whom all others claim direct succession, is strongly suggested by his reaction on being told that Mary Magdalen claimed to have a vision of Jesus during which they conversed. "Did Jesus really talk to a woman without *our* knowledge," asked Peter, to which the disciple Levi replied: "Peter you have always been hot tempered, if the Savior made her worthy, WHO ARE YOU to reject her?" On being told that Jesus had kissed Mary Magdalen on the lips Peter said; NEVER, Jesus would never be *caught* with a woman! Such attitude was echoed to me about 15 years ago when a catholic priest in commenting on a newspaper picture of Pope John Paul II holding a woman's hand said, "Who but a pope from Eastern Europe would be *caught* touching a woman?" The woman in this case was Mother Theresa !!! The use of the word *caught* is interesting. Does this mean that touching a woman is alright provided you don't get caught? In the name of the GOD, who made man and woman and intended them to be TWO as ONE, what kind of sickness in the minds of men would prompt this loathing for one half of the whole? It is a sickness all too prevalent today. And to those who are nay-sayers in regard to the veracity of the Gnostic texts one must enquire of them what is less believable about them than the synoptic gospels? Surely this dis-belief serves to

---

[5] The Gnostic Bible. Edited by Willis Barrstone and Marvin Myer.
[6] Elaine Pagels, Beyond Belief, The Secret Gospel of St. Thomas.. [Random House] 2000.

show how the systems and structures that sprang from the synoptic gospels and other texts of the New Testament are showing their power and resistance to change.

In her book "The Resurrection of Mary Magdalen" (2002) Jane Schaberg, a professor of Religion and Women's Studies at the University of Detroit Mercy, states that Mary Magdalen's witness of the Resurrection of Jesus, rather than being acclaimed as an act of devoted discipleship, was retold by the male writers of the scriptures as a story of the redemption of a repentant woman, in order to promote male dominance.

The pattern is a common one, she says, the powerful woman dis-empowered in order to be deemed a whore and to be remembered as whore-ish! For shorthand she coined the term HARLOTIZATION. I can assure the reader, such abusive perceptions and processes are alive and doing their dastardly wicked work, even as I write. If such treachery and disrespect is a sickness in the souls of men, then surely this sickness is mirrored in the souls of women and children.

AND SO IT IS.

Our explorations in the territories of exploitation, degradation, and abuse of women and children leaves no doubt about the injurious consequences inflicted on their spiritual, functional, emotional, and physical health, even on the many who have learnt how to cope as well as those who have greatly achieved. Overall, there is a dimming of the light and the energies of their sacred identities. In many other cases there is a rape of their felt connection to the source of all creative love. Women and children who have experienced abusive life situations often ask me why fathers, brothers, husbands, uncles, boyfriends, and others won't listen when they and their pain *beg* to be heard. Although I always try to fit my answer for children to age and level of development, nevertheless, the common root is the presence and persistence in the collective consciousness of what was planted there through the power of religious texts written by men, millennia ago which have since been the underpinning of cultural beliefs and behaviors.

In the year 2000, citing a report claiming 1 in 3 women world wide were the victims of beatings, predominately by husbands and other family members, the

United Nations declared domestic violence to be a global health problem. As far as I have been able to ascertain, U.N. programs designed to combat it have yet to be implemented.

AND YES, THERE IS MORE.

The imprimatur of unquestioned power vested in the male, deriving from and perpetuated by the religious and cultural institutions that enshrine it, is no longer just a matter of dimming the light on the souls and lives of women and children, and yes also on themselves.

IT IS NOW THREATENING THE EARTH'S ENVIORNMENT, THE OUTER ECOLOGY THAT SUSTAINS US ALL AND THE SUSTAINABILITY OF LIFE ON THIS PLANET.

The mindless belief that the Earth provides an endless source of treasures that can be mined and exploited for the financial gain of a few at the expense of the many is becoming a ruinous abuse. The consumerism that this begets and the garbage that ensues from it adds to the plunder. For the past fifty years or more, many have spoken out against this rape of Mother Earth. Their voices alas are effectively muzzled by those who promote "DEVELOPMENT" not only in the developed world but also in the so called developing world, which is becoming a euphemism for *more of the same.* Thankfully NOW, the clamor that is shouting STOP is becoming louder and less easy to ignore.[7] But this concern for the sustainability of Earth's environment, which we may refer to as OUTER ECOLOGY, in order to succeed must be indivisibly connected to concern for the INNER ECOLOGY of every human being which has here been defined as the interaction of the energies of body mind and soul that determine the health or otherwise of ones thoughts, feelings, and behavior towards self and interactions with other.

So let us now briefly explore signs that can tell us the degree of balance or imbalance that exists between the

---

[7] In 2006 a film documentary entitled *An Inconvenient Truth* whose text was predominantly authored by former Vice President of the United States Al Gore drew world wide attention to the urgency of this issue. He as well as the producer and director subsequently won the 2007 Oscar documentary award for this film.

energies of Inner and Outer Ecology, which knowledge is vital to understanding the state of our personal and societal health and which informs us of WHY we ARE the WAY we ARE.

# Epilogue

## *Quo Vadis*

There are in fact, some very heavy clues as to WHY and the extent to which dissonance exists between Inner and Outer Ecology. In the Western world fortunes are being made by many latter day seers and gurus who claim to know, and maybe they do, how to bring light and order out of the darkness and disorder that engulfs us both personally and societally. Books and other media on self help programs are best sellers and people are spending more on alternative therapies for all manner of conditions than medical insurance companies pay out every year to doctors and other health professionals. All of this is reaping the harvest of a prevailing desire to be free of fear and the depression and anxiety that accompanies it. All over the world people are suffering from a deep sense of disconnection from themselves and others. So pervasive is this sense of dis-connection and the violence, terror, and wars that it spawns, some programs have been specifically designed to assist nations in dealing with these plagues and down the line help in healing their wounds. Such is the intent of the Human Rights Program at the Carter Center of Emory University in Atlanta, Georgia. Founded by former President Jimmy Carter and his wife Roslyn, the aim is to assist fledgling democracies, and indeed those that are more mature, to understand and cope with the human rights abuses that devolve from this sense of personal and societal dis-connection. At a symposium held there in 1992 entitled "Coming to Terms with the Past," Robert Pastor, then director of the Center's Latin American and Caribbean program stated that: *"national reconciliation is a complex concept composed of two parts: first, society must be reconciled with its history, and second, both victims and violators must find a way to reconcile themselves to each other and get on with the business of constructing a just future."* Of the two, the second, of course, is the most difficult. MEMORY holds resentments forever, but as has already been pointed out, the Energies of these feelings CAN be CHANGED. President Carter in his address to the symposium said that "some element of forgiveness is absolutely necessary, because, as we should know by now, endless rounds of an 'eye for an eye' do not solve the problem." The importance of society being reconciled with itself was emphatically underscored by Dr. Karen Armstrong, author of "*The Battle for God*," in an article entitled, "Ghosts of Our Past"[1] which was published shortly after the tragedy of September 11, 2001 in New York City. Peace and the avoidance of tragedies similar to 9/11 she said, "depends on the First World developing a ONE WORLD mentality, which could do more (and I believe A LOT more) than First World fighter planes to create a safer and more just world for everyone." Such a scenario, of course, requires if not mandates that first world constituents examine their past and the role their history has played in present conflicts.

These observations about societies throughout the world needing to be reconciled with their history in order for them to construct a just future, not only confirms the dissonance between inner and outer ecology, but has a direct connection to the messages of this book. If we look to the statistics, those quoted here and the much more besides, what we find is that despite all efforts and programs to reconnect people with themselves and others, and despite some successes here and there, violence and other human behavior dysfunction is on the increase. A fact worthy of mention here, because it is a stark reminder of how miserably we are failing to stem the tide of negativity in WHY WE ARE THE WAY WE ARE, is that the number of children presenting to hospital emergency departments as Psychiatric emergencies is on the increase.[2]

So, what are we missing in our quests for inner and outer peace and the balance between Inner and Outer Ecology?

The journey we have made in this little book through the highways and byways of religious and cultural beliefs, attitudes, and behavior, leave little or no doubt that what we are missing is our failure to understand the profound imprinting these religious and cultural factors have left on

---

[1] Karen Armstrong, *Ghosts of Our Past* in Modern Maturity. Jan/Feb 2002.
[2] Karen Santucci. *The Epidemic of Psychiatric Diseases in Children.* The Yale New Haven Children's Hospital Physicians Letter, May 2000.

individuals and within the collective memory and consciousness of humanity. In this regard like so many of our approaches to problem solving we have been treating symptoms instead of causes, testifying to which is the failure of so many "remedial programs" that have cost and wasted billions. It is time to understand and NOT be afraid to acknowledge that whom we are and WHY WE ARE THE WAY WE ARE stretches far beyond and behind our own personal histories and experiences. It reaches to the furthest limits of humanity's own history and experience enshrined in its collective memory and consciousness. What we receive from this vast well are the energies of these memories and consciousness, and THAT is great and good news because energy frequencies can be changed. The how of doing this I have described in several other books and articles.[3] The message of this book is to apply the knowledge it and the other books contain to the correction of what needs to be addressed so that future generations are liberated to move on to the OMEGA point of ONE-NESS with GOD and CREATION.

The bottom line is that we must restore respect for women and the feminine and in particular be more attentive to nurturing the quality and the power of every mothers' thoughts, feelings, and situations during pregnancy. We know that the energies present at conception, during pregnancy and immediately following birth, are probably the greatest influences on the quality and texture of our entire life. The reason is that they set the energy frequencies from which we will respond to the hills and valleys of our lives. They are the nutrients of the soil within which the SOUL takes root and grows. It flourishes if the soil is tended with love and that special memory of connection that flows through the channel of being wanted, all of which becomes the infrastructure of its functional biology and giving to it, strong resilience to withstand life's testings. If the soil is needy for these nutrients or devoid of them, the energies of these memories and the damaged soul-full and emotional biology that flow from them will make resilience and acceptance of life's trials more difficult. In this regard I must emphasize that if every child was wanted, there would be a significant downward shift in

---

[3] For more information, visit www.drursulaanderson.com and www.andersonbeyondgenome.com.

psychological and psychiatric disorders which, as sicknesses of the soul are at the root of the sense and feeling of disconnection that spawns them.

Therefore it is more than just desirable, it should be mandatory to include programs that encourage positive energies in mothers-to-be as a central element in all Pre Natal Care. Some years ago (1986), I proposed such a program, but not being a money maker, it was still-born. The good news is that several similar programs have evolved over the last 10 years or so, particularly in Europe. But, what is needed is an organized full scale campaign to include the spiritual and self-regulatory procedures that promote healthy functioning of the trinity of mind, body, and soul as central ingredients of Pre Natal Care and then of School Curricula.

In a nutshell, establishing the sacred and the noble in personal and collective memory and consciousness requires that we enable parents, parents to be, and their children, to feel and to know the sacred and the noble within themselves, AND, within every other human being, truths which have floundered in the belief systems of religion and culture.

History and Experience inform us that to get societies and cultures engaged in these kinds of activities requires that we start at the grass roots level. How we do this has been described in detail in some of my other books. However above all it seems to me that NOW is the time to inject what we know and what needs to be done into the political and religious arenas. This belief coincides with and would give LIFE and LIGHT to a statement made in a document from Vatican II entitled "The Church in the Modern World,"

"The future of humanity lies with those who are strong enough to give coming generations REASON for living and REASON for hoping."

AMEN

# *Post Script*

The title of this book asks:

Who and Where is God?

Journeying through the pages and chapters of this book, which have brought us, you and I, to this post-script, the answer to this question clearly echoes over and over again.

God has been hijacked, imprisoned, and replaced by belief systems of religions and cultures created by men. So embedded are these beliefs in the personal and collective memories and consciousness of humanity, they have successfully buried deep beneath them the core messages of the GOD of ALL religions, which are, LOVE for GOD and for all fellow pilgrims on the journey of life, and who without exception yearn for, Compassion, Tolerance, and Justice. To discover the consequences of all of this, I invite you to return to the Prologue and then continue to read through the succeeding chapters, until you come full circle to this Post-Script. In doing so, you will come to know and to realize the power you have to change for the better the quality of the energies in the memories and consciousness in the message every new-born receives:

Welcome to Mother Earth and to the PAST that lies AHEAD
of you.

# *Appendix*

## Document 1

CENTRE UNESCO DE CATALUNYA     UNESCO     Generalitat de Catalunya

**THE CONTRIBUTION BY RELIGIONS TO THE CULTURE OF PEACE**
**LA CONTRIBUTION DES RELIGIONS À LA CULTURE DE LA PAIX**
**LA CONTRIBUCIÓN DE LAS RELIGIONES A LA CULTURA DE LA PAZ**
**LA CONTRIBUCIÓ DE LES RELIGIONS A LA CULTURA DE LA PAU**
BARCELONA, 12-18/12/1994

Declaration on the Role of Religion in the Promotion of a Culture of Peace

We, participants in the meeting, "The Contribution by Religions to the Culture of Peace," organized by UNESCO and the Centre UNESCO de Catalunya, which took place in Barcelona from 12 to 18 December, 1994,
Deeply concerned with the present situation of the world, such as increasing armed conflicts and violence, poverty, social injustice, and structures of oppression;
Recognizing that religion is important in human life;
Declare:

### OUR WORLD

1.     We live in a world in which isolation is no longer possible. We live in a time of unprecedented mobility of peoples and intermingling of cultures. We are all interdependent and share an inescapable responsibility for the well-being of the entire world.
2.     We face a crisis which could bring about the suicide of the human species or bring us a new awakening and a new hope.
We believe that peace is possible. We know that religion is not the sole remedy for all the ills of humanity, but it has an indispensable role to play in this most critical time.
3.     We are aware of the world's cultural and religious diversity. Each culture represents a universe in itself and yet it is not closed. Cultures give religions their language, and religions offer ultimate meaning to each culture. Unless we recognize pluralism and respect diversity, no peace is possible. We strive for the harmony which is at the very core of peace.
4.     We understand that culture is a way of seeing the world and living in it. It also means the cultivation of those values and forms of life which reflect the world-views of each culture. Therefore neither the meaning of peace nor of religion can be reduced to a single and rigid concept, just as the range of human experience cannot be conveyed by a single language.
5.     For some cultures, religion is a way of life, permeating every human activity. For others it represents the highest aspirations of human existence. In still others, religions are institutions that claim to carry a message of salvation.
6.     Religions have contributed to the peace of the world, but they have also led to division, hatred, and war.
We feel obliged to call for sincere acts of repentance and mutual forgiveness, both personally and collectively, to one another, to humanity in general, and to Earth and all living beings. Religious people have too often betrayed the high ideals they themselves have preached.

### PEACE

7.     Peace implies that love, compassion, human dignity, and justice are fully preserved.
8.     Peace entails that we understand that we are all interdependent and related to one another. We are all individually and collectively responsible for the common good, including the well-being of future generations.
9.     Peace demands that we respect Earth and all forms of life, especially human life. Our ethical awareness requires setting limits to technology. We should direct our efforts towards eliminating consumerism and improving the quality of life.
10.     Peace is a journey -- a never ending process.

## COMMITMENT

11. We must be at peace with ourselves; to achieve inner peace through personal reflection and spiritual growth, and to cultivate a spirituality which manifests itself in action.
12. We commit ourselves to support and strengthen the home and family as the nursery of peace.

In homes and families, communities, nations, and the world:

13. We commit ourselves to resolve or transform conflicts without using violence, and to prevent them through education and the pursuit of justice.
14. We commit ourselves to work towards a reduction in the scandalous economic differences between human groups and other forms of violence and threats to peace, such as waste of resources, extreme poverty, racism, all types of terrorism, lack of caring, corruption, and crime.
15. We commit ourselves to overcome all forms of discrimination, colonialism, exploitation, and domination and to promote institutions based on shared responsibility and participation. Human rights, including religious freedom and the rights of minorities, must be respected.
16. We commit ourselves to assure a truly humane education for all. We emphasize education for peace, freedom, and human rights, and religious education without fanaticism and exclusivism.
17. We commit ourselves to a civil society which respects environmental and social justice. This process begins locally and continues to national and trans-national levels.
18. We commit ourselves to work towards a world without weapons and to dismantle the industry of war.

## RELIGIOUS RESPONSIBILITY

19. Our communities of faith have a responsibility to encourage conduct imbued with wisdom, compassion, sharing, charity, solidarity, and love; inspiring one and all to choose the path of freedom and responsibility. Religions must be a source of helpful energy.
20. We will remain mindful that our religions must not identify themselves with political, economic, or social powers, so as to remain free to work for justice and peace. We will not forget that confessional political regimes may do serious harm to religious values as well as to society. We should distinguish fanaticism from religious zeal.
21. We will favor peace by countering the tendencies of individuals and communities to assume or even to teach that they are inherently superior to others. We recognize and praise the non-violent peacemakers. We disown killing in the name of religion.
22. We will promote dialogue and harmony between and within religions, recognizing and respecting the search for truth and wisdom that is outside our religion. We will establish dialogue with all, striving for a sincere fellowship on our earthly pilgrimage.

## APPEAL

23. Grounded in our faith, we will build a culture of peace based on non-violence, tolerance, dialogue, mutual understanding, and justice. We call upon the institutions of our civil society, the United Nations System, governments, governmental and non-governmental organizations, corporations, and the mass media, to strengthen their commitments to peace and to listen to the cries of the victims and the dispossessed. We call upon the different religious and cultural traditions to join hands together in this effort, and to cooperate with us in spreading the message of peace.

Figure 1

POLIOMYELITIS (paralytic) — by year, United States, 1965–1994

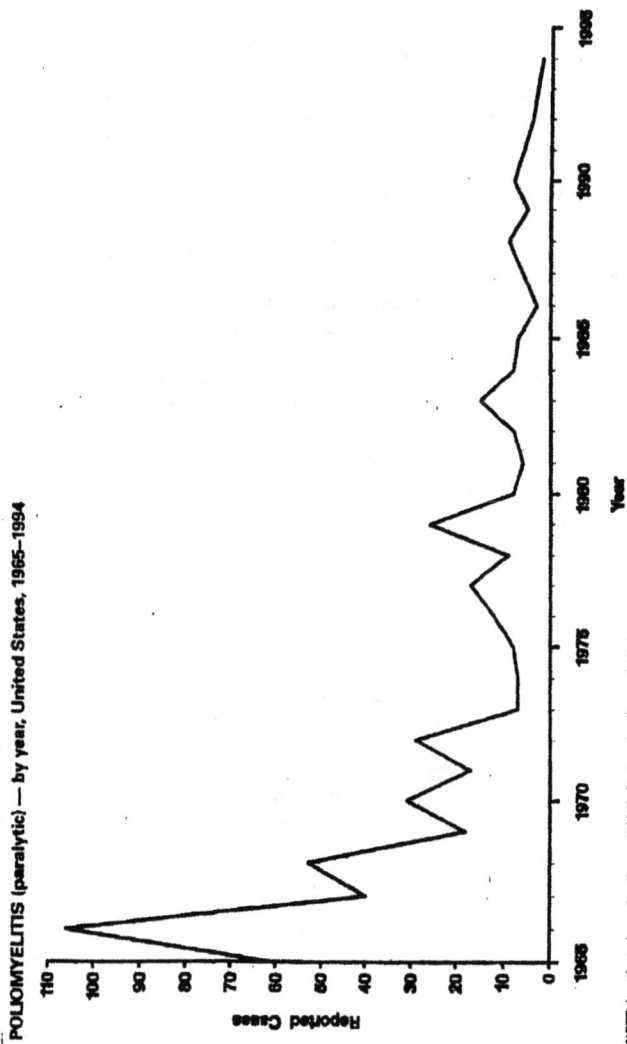

NOTE: Inactivated vaccine licensed 1955. Oral vaccine licensed 1961.

• Since 1980, all confirmed cases of indigenously acquired paralytic poliomyelitis in the United States have been vaccine-associated.

Figure 2

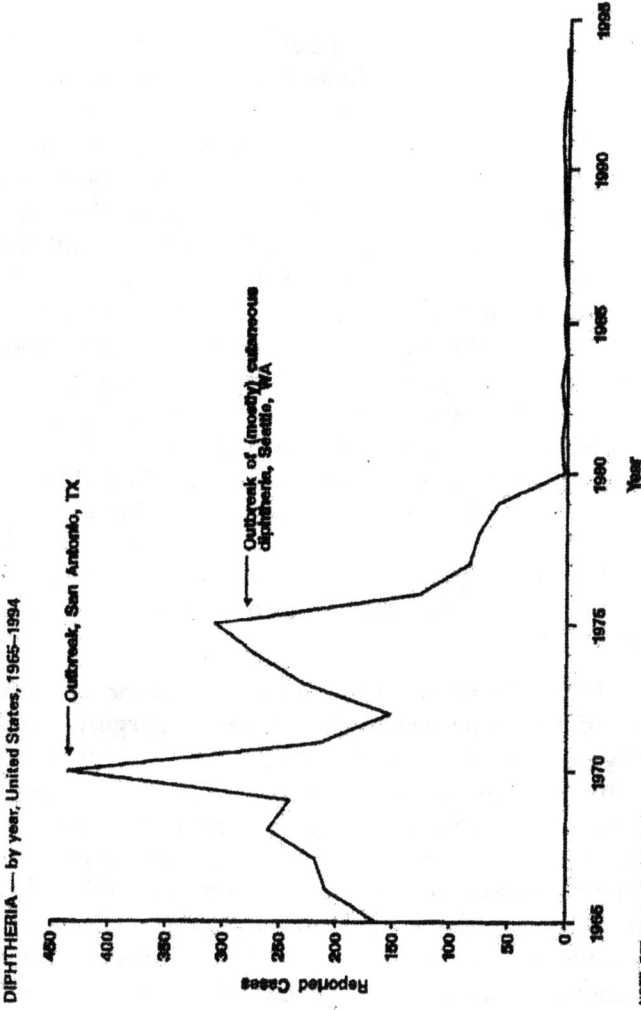

DIPHTHERIA — by year, United States, 1965–1994

NOTE: DTP vaccine licensed 1949.

*An ongoing epidemic of diphtheria is occurring in 14 of the 15 countries of the former Soviet Union. Two cases were reported among U.S. citizens residing in the former Soviet Union. No importation of diphtheria into the United States related to these outbreaks was reported in 1994.

# The Author's Post Note

This book, as indeed some of my others, took form out of my concern for those who have suffered in body, mind and soul, because they have been marginalized by cultural mores that are so often intertwined with religious beliefs.  My emphasis in this book was on women and children.  The dis-connection between tolerance, love and compassion, the tenets of all religions and their all too frequent absence in real life, has over the years led me to believe that these divine injunctions have been submerged by human interpretations of biblical texts designed to promote the status of religious leaders and invest them with power and control over their followers.  Therefore it was a great joy to discover and read Dr. Bart Ehrmans' book, *MISQUOTING JESUS, The Story Behind Who Changed the Bible and Why*, which was published in 2005, about a year and a half after I had completed this book in 2004.  The delay in publishing this book was due to injuries I received from a fall in 2004.

In his book, Dr. Ehrman describes how the biblical texts of the New Testament have undergone continual change in content and meaning.  One reason is that for centuries, until the advent of printing, their reproduction depended on scribes of varying capabilities often leading to inaccurate transcriptions.  Another reason is that religious leaders in charge of the texts would insert their own interpretations of the messages.  Consequently, what we use today are copies of endless copies whose messages derive in significant measure from a multiplicity of human input.  He further points out that the original texts of the four gospels in the New Testament Canon have not only been lost, but were written several decades after the death of Jesus.  These four were chosen as late as the fourth century from at least eight gospels now known to have been written.  We have since learned that the gospels not included give messages of the God within each human being and downplay the power of a few over the many, which is what we have lived with for two millennia.

His conclusions and indeed those of the several scholars whose recent books are now addressing similar issues, resonate with a theme that flows through this book, *"Who and Where is God?"* While acknowledging the many gifts with which religion has endowed humankind, there is no doubt it has also been used to create hierarchies of status and power who subjugate their followers with man made rules and laws that too often lead to the servitude of the many, particularly women and children, as well as allowing for abuse, violence and inter-religious wars.

These awareness's particularly in regard to the Judaic/Christian tradition are gushing forth at a time when there is a spiraling disaffection with organized religion. Consumerism and materialism are filling the void. It is my hope and belief that these are simply a bridge from man directed religious beliefs to a deeply felt connection to the eternal and life giving energy of the Holy Spirit, GOD, who is the source of ALL LIFE AND HEALING, in each and every human being.

Eventually and collectively this will free the world from its bondage to abuse and violence, which is the central message of this book.

Dr. Ursula Anderson

November, 2006

www.ingramcontent.com/pod-product-compliance
Lightning Source LLC
Chambersburg PA
CBHW071100090426
42737CB00013B/2401